Geraldine Brooks' Year of Wonders

Insight Text Guide By Virginia Lee

Copyright Page from the Original Book

Copyright © Insight Publications
First published in 2009.

Insight Publications Pty Ltd
89 Wellington Street
St Kilda VIC 3182
Australia
Tel: +61 3 9523 0044
Fax: +61 3 9523 2044
Email: books@insightpublications.com.au

www.insightpublications.com.au

Copying for educational purposes
The Australian *Copyright Act* 1968 (the Act) allows a maximum of one chapter or 10% of this book, whichever is the greater, to be copied by any educational institution for its educational purposes provided that the educational institution (or the body that administers it) has given a remuneration notice to Copyright Agency Limited (CAL) under the Act.

For details of the CAL licence for educational institutions contact:

Copyright Agency Limited
Level 15, 233 Castlereagh Street
Sydney NSW 2000 AUSTRALIA
Tel: +61 2 9394 7600
Fax: +61 2 9394 7601
Email: info@copyright.com.au

Copying for other purposes
Except as permitted under the Act (for example, any fair dealing for the purposes of study, research, criticism or review) no part of this book may be reproduced, stored in a retrieval system, or transmitted in any form or by any means without prior written permission. All inquiries should be made to the publisher at the address above.

National Library of Australia Cataloguing-in-Publication entry:
    Lee, Virginia.
    Geraldine Brooks' Year of wonders : insight text guide / Virginia Lee.
    1st ed.
    9781921088742 (pbk.)
    Insight text guide.
    Bibliography.
    For secondary school age.
    Brooks, Geraldine. Year of wonders.
A823.3

TABLE OF CONTENTS

CHARACTER MAP	i
OVERVIEW	ii
BACKGROUND & CONTEXT	1
GENRE, STRUCTURE & LANGUAGE	12
CHAPTER-BY-CHAPTER ANALYSIS	23
CHARACTERS & RELATIONSHIPS	63
THEMES, IDEAS & VALUES	90
DIFFERENT INTERPRETATIONS	112
QUESTIONS & ANSWERS	123
SAMPLE ANSWER	132
REFERENCES & READING	137

CHARACTER MAP

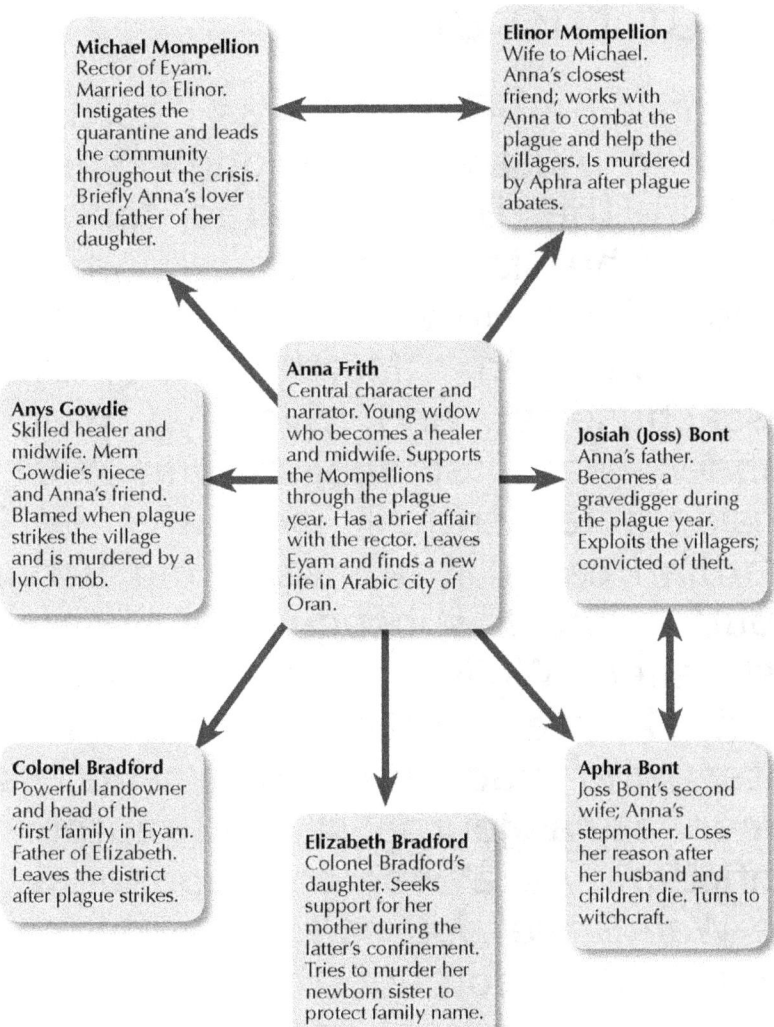

OVERVIEW

About the author

Geraldine Brooks was born and raised in Australia, although she has lived in the United States for many years. She is married to American author, Tony Horwitz, and divides her time between Martha's Vineyard, Massachusetts, and Sydney. *Year of Wonders* was first published in 2001 to considerable critical acclaim – *The Guardian* called it 'a staggering fictional debut' – and it subsequently became a best-seller. While it was Brooks' first novel, she was already an accomplished writer who had enjoyed a successful career as a journalist and author of nonfiction. As a war correspondent for *The Wall Street Journal*, she experienced the trouble spots of the Middle East, Bosnia and Somalia and developed a skilful eye for detail. Prior to *Year of Wonders*, Brooks wrote *Nine Parts of Desire: The Hidden World of Islamic Women* and *Foreign Correspondence: A Pen Pal's Journey from Down Under to*

All Over. Since the publication of *Year of Wonders,* Geraldine Brooks has written two further novels: *March* – which was awarded the Pulitzer Prize for Fiction – and *People of the Book.* Both deploy historical events in an imaginative and engaging way.

Synopsis

Year of Wonders is based on the true story of Eyam, a small village in the north of England, which made the remarkable decision to voluntarily quarantine itself when struck by plague in 1665. The text commences in autumn 1666, as Anna Frith, a young widow who serves the rector, Michael Mompellion, tries unsuccessfully to comfort her master on the recent loss of his wife, Elinor.

The narrative then reverts to the previous spring. A tailor from London, George Viccars, comes to the village to work and boards at Anna's house. Anna is grateful for the extra income, as her own husband, Sam, died in a mining accident the year before. She is also grateful for Viccars' good company and the generous interest he shows towards her two small sons. However, any relationship between them is cut short when Viccars sickens suddenly and dies of a mysterious and painful illness. Before his death, he begs that all of his belongings, as well as the garments he has made for the villagers, be burned. Anna is the only one who chooses to heed this advice.

Viccars has died of bubonic plague and the pestilence spreads rapidly throughout the village. The death toll mounts, and Anna is devastated when she loses both of her children in quick succession. As fear grips the community, some respond with violence and Mem and Anys Gowdie, the local healers, are targeted in a murderous attack. Michael Mompellion then takes control and uses his authority to implement the quarantine. After the defection of the Bradfords, the most powerful family in the area, responsibility for the welfare of the town falls heavily on the shoulders of Mompellion, his wife Elinor, and Anna herself.

The crisis brings out the best and the worst in the community. Some behave with great generosity and altruism, some with malice and greed. Joss Bont, Anna's father, is the worst of these. Having set himself up as a gravedigger, he shamelessly exploits the townspeople, and pays a grim price when he is indicted and judged guilty of theft. In contrast, Anna works closely with Elinor Mompellion in attempting to learn what they can from the Gowdies' herb knowledge in order to fight the plague. A strong bond is forged between them and Elinor entrusts Anna with the secret of her seduction as a young girl. Together the two women accomplish a great deal, including salvaging the fortunes of an orphaned child, Merry Wickford.

Finally, Mompellion determines to hold a 'great burning' and the villagers gather their possessions for a collective bonfire. This kills the fleas that are spreading the plague and the threat to the town abates. In the meantime, however, Aphra Bont has descended into madness. Having been harshly punished for her own attempts to exploit the villagers, she attacks and kills Elinor Mompellion in an act of deranged revenge.

This brings the narrative back to autumn 1666. Anna has a brief affair with the rector, but rejects him when she discovers the hurtful truth behind the Mompellion marriage. She accompanies Elizabeth Bradford to the Hall where she delivers the premature, illegitimate daughter of Mrs Bradford. Elizabeth tries to murder the newborn, but Anna stops her and offers to take the little girl. Mompellion helps Anna escape from the village, but rather than fleeing to Elinor's father's estate, as Mompellion has advised, Anna instead leaves England, sailing from Liverpool. She ultimately arrives in Oran, on the coast of North Africa. There she gives birth to Mompellion's daughter and finds a fulfilling new life as a healer, working alongside Ahmed Bey, the most illustrious doctor in the Arab world.

Character summaries

IN THE VILLAGE

Anna Frith

Narrator and protagonist of *Year of Wonders;* a young widow of 20, mother of two young sons. Has her own cottage, a flock of sheep and portion of land; supplements her small income by working in the mornings at the rectory, and occasionally serving at Bradford Hall.

Jamie and Tom Frith

Anna's two young sons by her deceased husband, Sam Frith.

Mem Gowdie

The elderly wise woman of the village, skilled with herbs and medicinals, as well as being an experienced midwife. Lives with her young niece, Anys, whom she has trained in 'physick'.

Anys Gowdie

Mem's niece and her natural successor; a skilled healer and midwife. Similar age to Anna. Has lived with

Mem since childhood, after the death of her own parents.

Josiah Bont

Anna's dissolute father. Lives with his second wife, Aphra, and their four children. Until he starts digging graves for the plague victims, has no obvious source of income. Spends much of his time at the tavern.

Aphra Bont

Joss Bont's second wife and mother to his four younger children; Anna's stepmother.

George Viccars

A young journeyman tailor from London who comes to work for Alexander Hadfield. About 28 years old.

Alexander and Mary Hadfield

Anna's neighbours; Alexander is the village tailor and Mary's second husband.

Christopher Unwin

The only surviving son of a prosperous mining family.

Alun Houghton
The Barmester: an elected officer who heads the Barmote Court. This assembly represents the interests of the miners (the Body of the Mine) and is the only semblance of law left in the village.

Jane Martin
A young Puritan girl who minds Anna's children when she is at work.

John and Urith Gordon
Villagers who are part of the lynching mob responsible for Anys' murder. John later becomes a flagellant.

Lib Hancock
Anna's childhood friend; married to a local farmer.

Mr Stanley
The Puritan (nonconformist) minister who preached in the village before Mompellion. Supports the decision to quarantine Eyam.

Merry Wickford
The young orphaned daughter of a Quaker miner.

AT THE RECTORY

Michael Mompellion
The young Anglican minister of Eyam; 28 years of age. Has worked in the village for three years and is married to Elinor. Emerges as leader of the community during the crisis.

Elinor Mompellion
Michael's wife, 25 years of age. Works actively in the village to support the community, and becomes Anna's closest friend.

AT THE HALL

Colonel Bradford
The owner of Bradford Hall and head of the 'first' family in the area. Fought on the side of the Royalists during the Civil War.

Mrs Bradford
Colonel Bradford's wife, and mother to Elizabeth. She is also the biological mother of Anna's adopted daughter, Aisha.

Elizabeth Bradford
Colonel and Mrs Bradford's daughter.

Maggie Cantwell
The Bradfords' cook. Has worked for the family for 18 years.

Brand
The pantry boy; works in the Bradfords' kitchen under Maggie Cantwell's supervision.

IN ORAN

Ahmed Bey
An elderly Arab doctor, the most eminent and skilled physician on Africa's Barbary Coast. Takes on Anna as his assistant and she lives with him officially as one of his wives.

Aisha and Elinor Frith
Anna's daughters.

1

BACKGROUND & CONTEXT

Historical and social setting

Year of Wonders is set in a small village in Derbyshire, in the north of England, in the second half of the 17th century. This period in English history is known as the Restoration. From 1641 to 1651, England had been laid waste by civil war between the Royalists, who supported the king, and the Parliamentarians, who opposed the principle of absolute monarchy. After the execution of Charles I in 1649 and Parliament's final victory two years later, the royal family went into exile and the Commonwealth was established under the leadership of Oliver Cromwell. References to these tumultuous events are sprinkled throughout the novel. Colonel Bradford, who fought for the Royalists, is described as an 'intelligent soldier who had led his men with uncommon valour' (p.57) – though that leadership is conspicuously absent in his response to the disaster that subsequently grips Eyam. By contrast, Michael Mompellion's father was a curate who had fought on the side of Parliament. In a sad irony that demonstrates the capricious unpredictability of war, he was accidentally killed by a party of his own men.

During this period, the monopoly of the Church of England was also challenged. Cromwell was a Puritan and supported a plainer, more conservative form of Protestant doctrine. Puritans believed that the Church of England continued to borrow too heavily from the practices and traditions of the Roman Catholic Church and, similarly, had lost its 'purity' of vision. They argued for greater simplicity of worship, eschewing many of the more traditional aspects of the Anglican service, such as the Book of Common Prayer. In *Year of Wonders,* Anna comments that the Puritan Thomas Stanley's Sabbath had been 'severe' and his church had been 'a cheerless place, innocent of lace or polished brass and stinting even in the beauty of its prayers' (p.100). Puritans led strict, abstemious lives and the rigidity of their beliefs alienated many in England.

In 1660, Charles II returned from Holland and was restored to the throne. His reign was the antithesis of the austere rule of the Puritans. Under Charles' patronage, the arts and sciences flourished. Theatres were reopened and drama was revived – women were even allowed on stage for the first time. The times were more liberal, more inclusive and increasingly secular. Charles II's reign was also characterised by an intellectual curiosity that saw the establishment of the Royal Society in 1662 to explore and advance the study of natural science. In the future, scientific truths would be validated by the empirical evidence that emerged from practical experimentation, rather than being located in superstition or prejudice. Brooks observes, in the interview that accompanies the text, that the Restoration was a 'fluid' time where the 'ancient certainties' of both monarchy and church were under challenge. Having lived through unprecedented political turmoil, the citizens of England were both resilient and adaptable: 'Change was their norm' (p.318).

Again, there are a number of references in the text alluding to the subtle shift in values taking place. Though these shifts are more evident in the large towns, even a remote community like Eyam is not entirely untouched by the changes. For example, Anna describes a more relaxed attitude with regard to the clothing worn: 'For all the years of my childhood, when the Puritans held sway here, we wore for our outer garments only what they called the Sadd Colours – black for preference, or the dark brown called Dying Leaf' (pp.48–9). She explains that 'brighter hues' had crept back into the wardrobes of those who could afford new clothes. Otherwise, even Anys would not have been sufficiently brazen as to flaunt herself in the scarlet dress that George Viccars had made for her. Not only is Anna startled by its dazzling colour; she also notes that the neckline is 'cut low as a doxy's' (p.49) – a far cry from the Puritans' insistence on plain, modest attire.

However, some things had not changed. England was still a society deeply divided by class. Power resided in the hands of the nobility and the gentry – the wealthy landowners. England was an agrarian, pre-industrial society. While there had been some population shift to London, the majority still lived and worked in the country, usually farming the land. Some owned the freehold to small farms; most leased their land from the large landowners as tenant farmers. These class divisions are evident in *Year of Wonders.* Eyam is a community of farmers and lead miners. While most of the villagers are self-sufficient, in many cases, such as the Mowbrays, there is real poverty. At the other end of the social spectrum, there are the Bradfords. The family has lived in the Hall and presided over the town for generations. They are answerable to no one in the immediate vicinity. As they leave Eyam, 'Men doffed their caps and women curtsied, just as we had always done, simply because that was what we had always done' (p.116). Mompellion's argument that responsibility accompanies power and privilege is completely lost on Colonel Bradford. By contrast, the earl at Chatsworth House, a little further afield, *does* use his wealth generously to support the villagers through the crisis.

Religious divisions

The religious divisions of the Reformation were still a feature of society. Europe was on the cusp of a more enlightened age, yet retained many of the prejudices and intolerances of the previous century. In England, a Roman Catholic monarch was on the throne, but the majority of the population was Protestant. The continuing, though discredited, presence of the Puritans ensured an uncomfortable division within Christian ranks. The text refers to many of these tensions, apparent even in a relatively isolated community like Eyam:
- The young Quaker family, the Wickfords, live on the outskirts of the village. Their 'queer faith' has caused them to be persecuted and driven off their own land further in the

south. While they are viewed with general reserve by the people of Eyam, 'at least they didn't have to fear their ricks being fired or their poultry poisoned' (p.172).
- Thomas Stanley, the resident priest before Michael Mompellion, is regarded as a 'dissenter' or 'nonconformist'. He is one of hundreds of Puritan ministers who resigned from their pulpits in 1662, refusing to endorse the order from Parliament to use the Book of Common Prayer. Rigorous laws protect the established Church of England from the influence of nonconformists, so that they cannot 'stir up differences' (p.100).
- Viewed with equal suspicion are the 'papists' – Roman Catholics – whose legacy still lingers over a century after the schism with the Vatican. There are still many Roman Catholics living in England, heartened no doubt by the fact that the reigning royal family is of their faith. Yet even Mompellion uses a pejorative tone when he refers to their practices.

Bubonic plague

The Restoration was a period of relative peace although, internally, the English population experienced real trauma with the last significant outbreak of plague in 1665–66, followed by the Great Fire of London in 1666. The 'Black Death' – bubonic plague – was a virulent pandemic that had ravaged Europe throughout the centuries. Major outbreaks dated from the 14th century when the plague claimed at least 30 per cent of Europe's population, with profound social and economic ramifications.

The Black Death was a deadly bacterial infection spread by fleas that had fed on an infected host – usually rats. The infected fleas then transmitted the disease to humans. One of the first symptoms of the disease was a rosy red rash in the shape of a ring on the skin. Victims suffered high fever, headache, nausea and vomiting. The infection also caused swellings, or buboes, in the lymph nodes, which subsequently burst, oozing pus and blood. Death usually occurred within a few days. No one knew what caused the plague or how it was spread. Consequently there were few strategies to deal with it and fleeing the site of the contagion seemed to be a logical option. Certainly it was the most generally adopted option for those with the means to do so.

The London outbreak in 1665 is thought to have been spread from Holland by trading ships sailing back and forth. Up to 100 000 people died in the Great Plague of London – approximately 20 per cent of the population. In *Year of Wonders,* George Viccars' disparaging image of the city as 'a corpulent man trying to fit himself into the jerkin he wore as a boy' (p.27) highlights the massive overcrowding that characterised the poorer parishes of London. This of course helped the disease to spread. Those who were able, including the royal family, left for the comparative safety of the country. The inevitable panic that accompanied the mass evacuation from the city is also vividly described in the text: 'Innumerable men on horseback, wagons, and carts bulging with baggage

... everyone capable of leaving the city is doing so or plans to do it' (pp.59–60). In September 1666, the Great Fire of London destroyed much of central London, but also cleansed the city slums of many of the rat hosts. The plague began to abate soon after.

Lead mining in Eyam

Eyam, Derbyshire, lies in the centre of the Peak District which is known for its rich lead deposits. In the 17th century, lead was used extensively in the building trade. It was also used for piping and water storage, as well as military purposes – lead shot was used as ammunition in muskets. Brooks has woven details of the miners' lives and customs into the novel. Ancient law allowed an individual to claim a lead seam, irrespective of whose land it lay upon. A claimant then had nine weeks to work the claim and produce a set amount of ore, after which the mine was effectively theirs. A tax known as 'the King's Dish' was paid to the Crown, and the miner had to continue to work the claim. If he was unable to do so, through illness or death, another miner had the right to 'nick his stowe'; that is, to make a counter-claim to the mine.

This was a pragmatic system, designed to maximise the resources of the land and guarantee the Crown's claim to all mineral rights. However, it left no room for sentiment or generosity, as the case of Merry Wickford demonstrates. She can only retain the title to her father's mine if she is able to mine the lead seam; otherwise, within the designated period of nine weeks, she will lose the claim to David Burton. Lead mining was difficult and hazardous work, as Sam Frith's death testifies, but it could also be lucrative for those prepared to take the risks.

GENRE, STRUCTURE & LANGUAGE

Genre: Historical fiction

Year of Wonders is an historical novel inspired by the true story of the 'plague village' in the 17th century. In her Afterword and the subsequent interview, Brooks explains the genesis of her novel and the extent to which she has drawn on the remarkable and poignant story of Eyam. Some of the characters in the novel are based, at least in part, on real-life personalities. She has also borrowed from the 'wealth of anecdote' (p.308) available, including the report that the plague was carried from London by an infected bolt of cloth. The novel is carefully researched and Brooks has incorporated a wealth of detail that vividly recreates rural England of the 1660s. Descriptions of customs and practices from the period, many of which would be unfamiliar to a modern audience, establish a powerful sense of time and place.

While *Year of Wonders* is primarily historical fiction, there are also elements of mystery, romance and allegory. Despite the fact that the outcome for most in the community is a foregone conclusion, Brooks generates suspense in several ways. The stories of particular characters, like Joss and Aphra Bont, have a chilling urgency and the audience is impelled to read on to discover their respective fates. Nor are things always as they seem – secrets are exposed as the narrative unfolds. The emotional core of the narrative – the relationship between Anna, Elinor and Michael Mompellion – provides an element of romance, but here Brooks deliberately foils readers' expectations. The ending of the novel does not conform to a conventional pattern, but takes a less predictable direction.

Finally, the extended metaphor of the plague adds a layer of complexity to the literal drama being played out in Eyam. As well as absorbing historical fiction, *Year of Wonders* can also be read as a grim warning about how communities can destroy themselves from within. The plague becomes a metaphor for infection, a polluting contaminant that destroys the mind and spirit as well as the body. Just as bacteria contaminate the bloodstream, so too does fear infect the people, who are swift to abrogate rationality in favour of panic and superstition. The literal destruction of the community is accompanied by a figurative death as the social framework starts to implode, and trust, goodwill, even respect for the law, begin to break down.

Structure

Year of Wonders essentially has a circular structure, within which the narrative follows a linear trajectory. The novel commences in autumn 1666, after the plague has devastated the town, and then takes the reader back to the previous spring. We follow the awful deterioration of events throughout the year before returning full circle to autumn 1666. The novel concludes with an epilogue which moves forward three years. This structure enables the protagonist to look back on events with the added advantage of hindsight and retrospectively examine the crisis that has threatened Eyam. Not only is it a critical time in the life of the village; it also corresponds to a period of formative growth in Anna's own life.

The chapter titles act as a summary, recording the passage of time and charting the way in which the plague year runs its course. This structure is also an effective way of engaging the audience and generating dramatic tension. For example, in the opening chapter Anna refers to a calamity that the town has suffered in the preceding year and alludes to some of its consequences. Questions hang in the air and there is just enough information offered to whet our curiosity.

Language

The historical setting of a small mining village in the 17th century informs Brooks' language choices. So too does the 'voice' of her narrator: in this case, an independent and intelligent observer of events, whose tone becomes increasingly confident and aware. Brooks has effectively captured the rhythms and cadences of a more formal time in history. This gives the language of the text, including the dialogue, an authenticity, evoking the flavour of a bygone age. For example, her characters do not use contractions when they speak. Some of their vocabulary has disappeared from everyday speech; for example, words such as 'unlovely' or 'amiss'. Other descriptions, like 'contagion', are rarely used today. Throughout the narrative, the old subject/object pronouns 'thou' and 'thee' are often employed instead of the more familiar 'you'. There are also a number of specialist terms that flesh out the mining and agricultural background.

Brooks' extensive use of metaphor is worth noting and her descriptions of people and places contain many memorable images. The hands of the young London guest of the Bradfords 'fluttered from lace cuffs like white moths' (p.59), suggesting a weak and ineffectual personality. Anna's description of the village as 'a thin thread of dwellings, unspooling east and west of the church' (p.11) confirms the central place of religion in the lives of these people, while the picture of the residents of Eyam living 'all aslant' on the 'steep flank' (p.11) of White Peak brings to mind their vulnerability.

The novel contains lyrical descriptive passages that establish context and delineate Anna's relationship to the landscape, often directly reflecting her emotional state: 'that morn the air was rich with summer's loamy fragrance. It was a morning fit for the contemplation of new beginnings' (p.33). The pastoral serenity of the surrounding countryside contrasts sharply with the graphic accounts of the devastation wrought by the plague within the village. While the catalogue of horrors is deliberately designed to unnerve, even shock, the audience, Brooks avoids the use of gratuitous detail. The result is an impressive equilibrium that is maintained between the polarities of survival and hope on the one hand, and the cruel realities of the period on the other. Brooks' carefully plotted imagery comes into play here. Juxtaposed against the images of death and waste – for example, rotting apples – is the pervasive motif of new life.

Brooks makes a distinction between the religious abstraction promulgated by priests and ministers during the crisis and the tangible comfort that can be offered in *this* life, however bleak it may sometimes seem. Mompellion exhorts his congregation to believe in the resurrection of Christ and their own rebirth after death, but ultimately even he loses faith in this promise. In contrast, the delivery of new life, whether it is a baby lamb or the birth of a child, provides true evidence of the tenacity of existence and acts as an antidote to the pain and loss that dominate the narrative.

Significance of the title

'The Year of Wonders', the poem at the beginning of the text, was written by John Dryden in 1666 and refers to the Great Plague of London. It is from this poem that Brooks has chosen her title. Dryden expresses the prevailing view that the pestilence is a punishment sent by a wrathful God. Those few who are spared must consider the 'searching judgments' implied. The plague itself then is the first 'wonder' – in the biblical sense of the word – similar to the plague sent to the Egyptians as retribution for their treachery.

Brooks' explanation of her choice of title is pertinent. She reminds us of the way in which language and its meaning can change with time. Dryden's 17th-century audience would have interpreted 'wonder' as something both powerful and terrible, rather than simply 'strange' or 'remarkable'. The description evokes the religious perspective of the period and the accepted belief in an all-powerful God who is more than capable of wreaking devastation on his people. Furthermore, God's actions are seen to have purpose, irrespective of how cruel and incomprehensible they may appear, and it is not for the faithful to challenge this. Anna, however, does come to reject this general view. By the end of the text, she admits that her faith – 'that flimsy, tattered thing' – has not only been tested, but effectively destroyed (p.301). She cannot accept or rationalise the tragedy she has lived through on religious grounds. Rather, she questions whether, in fact, God has had anything to do with it at all. Ironically, it is Anna's own transformation, from an inexperienced and unlettered servant to an educated woman of great skill and understanding, that is one of the true 'wonders' in the modern sense of the word.

What other 'wonders' come out of the 'annus mirabilis'? A few possibilities are:
- the extraordinary heroism shown by the people of Eyam in containing the spread of the disease
- the close friendship that develops between Anna and Elinor
- the way in which the crisis defuses religious divisions of the past
- the more extreme and bizarre manifestations of social distress
- perhaps most miraculous of all, the 'wonders' (p.287) of life's resilience and its ability to regenerate, despite suffering and adversity.

Narrative point of view

Year of Wonders is narrated by the protagonist, Anna Frith, and it is her story as well as Eyam's that unfolds. The novel is written exclusively from her perspective; Anna's is the only voice we hear throughout. She is generally a reliable narrator who tries to be as fair and objective as she can. Several facts place her at the epicentre of events and therefore she is well positioned to chronicle Eyam's sad history. The plague first spreads from her cottage, a 'starburst of death' (p.156). Her status as servant to the rector, with close links both to the village and to Bradford Hall, affords her access to a number of crucial conversations and incidents. Similarly, her personal relationship with both of the Mompellions provides her with information that could otherwise not be revealed to the reader, and as Elinor's confidante and Michael Mompellion's lover, she is entrusted with their secrets.

Nevertheless, Anna cannot know everything. Her understanding of events and other characters is inevitably limited by perspective and circumstance. She herself acknowledges the limitations of any one person's comprehension: 'How little we know, I thought, of the people we live among' (p.155). Like any character, Anna can also be driven by her passions and loyalties; for example, her fierce allegiance to Elinor leads her to judge the rector harshly at the end.

Anna's voice is a strong one: incisive, open-minded, and reflective. While she grows in assertiveness and wisdom, she remains honest with regard to her own shortcomings, and is often critical of the times when he wishes she had behaved differently. Of all of those who interact with her, Elinor is the character best positioned to balance Anna's self-effacing view of herself.

CHAPTER-BY-CHAPTER ANALYSIS

Leaf-fall, 1666: Apple-picking time

Summary: *As Anna Frith serves the rector, Michael Mompellion, she reflects on past events: the death of her husband, Sam, the death of Elinor Mompellion, the grief of the village; Elizabeth Bradford comes to the rectory on behalf of her mother, but Mompellion turns her away; Mompellion remains grief-stricken over the loss of Elinor.*

In this opening chapter, readers are introduced to two of the main characters, Anna Frith and Michael Mompellion. We learn that the village in which they live has experienced immense trauma over the previous year, and that Elinor Mompellion has merely been one of many in 'that long procession of dead' (p.9). The retrospective voice refers to the people's exhaustion and grief; even the main street through the village has been reclaimed by Nature. Nevertheless, though the grassed-over path attests to the lack of traffic, the stubborn sprouting of a small walnut sapling symbolises new life and intimates that the worst may be over for the people of Eyam.

The relationship between Anna and Mompellion, though officially that of master and servant, is a slightly ambiguous one. Anna admits that a servant 'has no right to stay, once she's dismissed' (p.4), yet she takes the initiative in a way that arguably exceeds her designated role. Anna's motives for serving Mompellion so diligently and thanklessly are the logical extension of her love for Elinor. Nevertheless, the rhetorical question that hangs on the air – 'Why else would I do it, after all?' (p.9) – suggests there may be more to the connection than she is able to admit. Anna and the rector are united in their hostility towards Elizabeth Bradford and the latter's unwelcome appearance stirs Mompellion from his apathy. His refusal to attend the ailing Mrs Bradford is partially due to his anger at the family's earlier abrogation of duty. It also becomes obvious that Mompellion is suffering a crisis of faith that has left him bitter and disillusioned. God has been 'a poor listener' (p.17) and Mompellion's deliberate dropping of the Bible reveals his contempt for its message.

This chapter introduces the motif of rotten apples. Apple-picking time is no longer the rich season of bounty and contentment of happier times. The 'thick, sweet' (p.3) smell of rotting apples, which Anna once loved, has now become inextricably associated with the memory of death – whether it be Sam Frith's or that of the plague victims: 'If there's one thing I can't stand anymore, it's the scent of a rotting apple' (p.6). Rather than evoking abundance, it has come to represent waste.

Q What are your first impressions of Anna? Of Mompellion?

Q How does Brooks establish the social and historical context?

Spring, 1665: Ring of roses

Summary: *George Viccars comes to board at Anna's house; a friendship develops between the two; a box of cloth arrives from London; Viccars makes his attraction to Anna clear; however, he falls gravely ill and dies within 24 hours.*

Anna enjoys the companionship and laughter that Viccars brings to her home, and appreciates the kindness he shows towards her small son, Jamie. Viccars brings the wider world into Anna's cottage. Like most villagers of her time, Anna has not been further afield than the neighbouring market town. Tales of distant lands and the Arab world, like the Muslim merchant with 'four wives all veiled' (p.26), have an exotic appeal and foreshadow Anna's future. Bawdy stories of London and the licentious court of Charles II reinforce the differences between the tone of the restored monarchy and the strict Puritan ethos. When Viccars entertains her with anecdotes of the lecherous behaviour that has become commonplace in the city, Anna's instinctive open-mindedness is evident. She looks beyond the outcome to the cause and resists judgement. Regarding the women who resort to prostitution, she observes: 'But before I blamed, I would like to know the extent of her choices in the hard world' (p.28). Genuine curiosity and a thirst for information override conventional indignation.

At the rectory, we are introduced to the third main character, Elinor Mompellion. Anna is in awe of the idyllic life that Elinor appears to have and the bond between the two women is already strong. Elinor has discovered Anna's hunger to learn and responded generously, 'shovelling' knowledge Anna's way 'as vigorously as she spaded the cowpats into her beloved flower beds' (p.36). Under Elinor's guidance and encouragement, Anna's education has begun. At this stage though, Anna *does* resist her friend's herb knowledge. As a single woman, Anna is far more vulnerable to society's censorious scrutiny than is Elinor, and she has previously witnessed the unfavourable consequences when unprotected women 'meddle' in medicinals (p.38). The domestic tasks that Anna performs allow her imagination to roam. Again, her destiny is foreshadowed as she tries to imagine life 'under a hot sun and a strange God' (p.41).

When Anna discovers that Viccars is gravely ill, her healing instincts come to the fore. She nurses him without hesitation, oblivious to her own danger. Under the skin of Viccars' face bloom shapes 'like rings of rose petals' (p.42). These red circular blotches are 'plague tokens' and they become one of the enduring images in the text. Brooks also draws attention to the hands of her characters. George Viccars has 'beautiful hands, soft save for the one callused place toughened by a lifetime of needle pricks' (p.44). By contrast, Mompellion's are roughened and large, 'the hard hand of a labouring man rather than the limp, white paw of a priest' (p.45). Both represent a lifetime of industry and experience. Anna laments the waste that accompanies death: the waste of skills, of love, the loss of all of the components that make up a productive life.

Q How does a different side to Mompellion emerge in this chapter?

The thunder of his voice

Summary: *Mompellion urges Anna to burn Viccars' belongings, as well as the garments he has made; Viccars' customers, including Anys Gowdie, reject this advice; Anna visits Anys to discuss her relationship with Viccars; Anna serves at the Bradfords' table as they entertain a large party, including the Mompellions; talk is of the plague that has overtaken London.*

All of the power structures in the 17th century are invested in men, and once women marry they effectively become the property of their husbands. Anys Gowdie resists the societal imperative to marry, dismissing marriage as an institution designed to oppress women. While 'her fornication and her blasphemy branded her a sinner' according to the religious and social conventions of the day (p.55), Anys remains indifferent to public opinion. She values her freedom too much to relinquish it. Anys shrewdly observes that Anna has also grown to appreciate her independence, despite the difficulties imposed by her widowed state.

Key point

One of the strongest values underpinning the society in which Anna lives is patriarchy and this chapter explores the issue in some detail.

The discussion with Anys causes Anna to reappraise women's roles. As she watches the Hancock women wearily following their husbands, the drudgery of working women's lives is very clear. For the first time, she judges the scene 'through Anys's eyes' (p.55). The contrast between the grandeur of Bradford Hall and the humble subsistence of the villagers could not be more marked, yet Mrs Bradford is no less a victim of the patriarchal society than her less privileged contemporaries. Her husband is an arrogant bully who holds his whole household to ransom. In particular, he treats his wife with great cruelty. While he was happy to pocket her sizeable dowry, he never lets an opportunity pass 'to disparage her connections or slight her understanding' (p.57). Mrs Bradford is belittled in public and has become brittle and nervous as a result. When she is desperate and ill-advised enough to seek consolation outside her unhappy marriage, she pays a heavy price.

The Bradfords' guest reports the alarming news from London. The plague has taken over the city and everyone who is able is fleeing to the perceived safety of the country. The young man describes scenes of chaos and panic that foreshadow the tragedy that will strike Eyam. This leads to a heated debate between Colonel Bradford and Michael Mompellion about the morality of trying to outrun the infection. Mompellion, motivated by altruism and a strong sense of social responsibility, is passionate in his argument that it is essential to contain the spread. Bradford, equally adamant, but driven by self-interest, insists that it is only prudent to flee the danger. Ironically, the physicians and barber-surgeons are 'the fleetest of foot' in leaving the capital, their 'clear prescription' offering little support to the idea of quarantine (p.62). The fact that the Anglican ministers have been nearly as quick to quit London suggests that few of Mompellion's colleagues share his principles. These principles will be sorely tested in the months to come.

Q What does Mompellion mean when he says, 'Perhaps they might believe that God now is preaching to the city, and what needs add their small utterance to the thunder of His voice?' (p.63).

Rat-fall

Summary: Anna spends a happy time with her sons; an infestation of fleas arrives with the cooler weather; Anna's neighbours, the Hadfields, are struck down by plague; Anna's younger son, Tom, dies soon after.

The serene autumn that Anna enjoys with her sons is the last untroubled memory that she will have for a long time. On the afternoon that Jamie helps her to deliver a baby lamb, she is reminded of the continual interplay of life and death. Shortly after the lamb's birth, as she sits nursing Tom, she watches a dragonfly ruthlessly kill a passing wasp: 'So it goes, I thought idly. A birth and a death, each unlooked for' (p.68). These opposites will be played out, over and over, in Eyam in the immediate future.

When Anna unexpectedly encounters Michael Mompellion, she sees a different side to him. Rather than the aloof figure she is used to, he is more than comfortable to take off his boots and relax with her little boys. He talks to Anna of the 'ordinary, daily miracles of creation' (pp.69–70) and invites her to consider the many patterns of cyclical renewal that characterise the natural world. For Anna, the greatest miracles are her children. However, while Jamie's shower of rose petals highlights Mompellion's insight that it is the small, luminous moments that contribute joy and meaning to existence, it is also a reminder of life's more sinister undercurrents. Rose petals evoke the plague and the rosy rings will shortly bloom on the delicate skin of Anna's sons. The juxtaposition of life's polarities – its happiness and promise versus its fragility – is brought home to her in the most brutal possible way. Anna acknowledges this tension when Tom is dying: 'fear of losing him had marched beside that love, every moment of the short time I had him with me' (p.78).

Q What is the significance of Anna's statement regarding Anys: 'I thought that she could teach me much about how to manage alone as a woman in the world' (p.73).

Q What do we learn of the treatment of the sick in the 17th century?

Sign of a witch

Summary: Anna is overwhelmed with grief following Jamie's death; the town grapples with a mounting death toll; Mem and Anys Gowdie are targeted in a shocking display of mob violence that culminates in Anys being hanged;

order is only restored when Mompellion arrives on the scene.

As her 'merry little boy' (p.81) fights for his life, Anna is appreciative of the comfort brought by Elinor Mompellion and Anys Gowdie. The latter accurately predicts that 'Your arms will not be empty forever. Remember that when the way looks bleak to you' (p.84). Anna's desolation takes her to the churchyard where she spends much time, not with the 'beloved dead', but sitting by the older graves. Again, the image of the briar roses, tumbling 'in a bright profusion' over these ancient graves (p.87), acts as a reminder of the cyclical polarities of life and death. Anna's grief leads her to some of the great existential questions. Why are death and suffering so arbitrary? How is it possible to reconcile the image of a just and merciful God with the suffering of the innocent? It is the beginning of her loss of faith. The stone Celtic cross, representative of a bygone time and looming over the Christian monuments like 'some uneasy foreign visitor' (p.87), symbolises the enduring power of religious conviction. However, it also demonstrates the ephemeral nature of belief systems and the way in which one is, sooner or later, superseded by another.

Superstition lurks just below faith. The villagers' readiness to believe in the Devil as the architect of the plague goes hand in hand with their susceptibility to charms and potions. (It is revealing that even Elinor Mompellion is prepared to pass on the Florentine doctors' recommendation of a dried toad over the heart.) When grief turns to rage, the impulse to lash out and blame quickly follows. The calamity exposes the ugly underbelly of this small community: the murderous attack on the Gowdie women demonstrates the way in which blind irrationality can overtake common decency. Mompellion's authority is finally able to intimidate the mob into contrite submission, but too late to save Anys' life. His leadership of Eyam dates from this point.

Key point

The first response to the crisis is a negative one. In their fear and panic, the villagers look for a scapegoat and turn on each other.

Q To what extent does Anys inflame the temper of the mob? Discuss her response.

Venom in the blood

***Summary:** Mem Gowdie dies shortly after her niece; remorse over the murders permeates the village; Mompellion delivers a passionate sermon, exhorting the villagers to quarantine themselves in order to contain the plague.*

The increasing isolation of the town is evidenced by the lack of legal redress over the Gowdie deaths. Eyam is already being shunned by the outside world. There is, however, a grim justice in the fact that most who are guilty are struck down by the 'venom in the blood' (p.102). At the same time, the crisis is creating unexpected alliances. Mompellion confers with Mr Stanley, the previous incumbent and a 'dissenter', as to his proposed course of action and Stanley proves to be an invaluable ally.

Mompellion deploys all of his eloquence to persuade the villagers to quarantine Eyam. Indeed, his delivery is so serene and engenders such a sense of communal warmth that he is more than halfway into the sermon that seals their fates before the congregation grasps his true intent: 'He intoxicated us with his words, lifting and carrying us away into a strange ecstasy' (p.101). Rather than emphasising its punitive aspects, Mompellion describes the plague as a 'gift' and a 'casket of gold' (p.102). He urges his listeners to emulate Christ's example and be guided by love of their fellow human beings. By implication, those who have sinned have an opportunity to redeem themselves. Mompellion's ardent commitment to the strategy is compelling and he convinces the majority to 'trust in God to perform His wonders' (p.104). Those who remain sceptical, like the Bonts, have their own selfish reasons to comply with the Sunday oath.

> **Key point**
>
> In orchestrating the quarantine of the village, Michael Mompellion assumes authority over the crisis.

Q How valid is Mompellion's clear manipulation of the townspeople?

Wide green prison

Summary: Despite Mompellion's pleas, the Bradfords quit the Hall, refusing to take their servants; the villagers look to Mompellion for leadership; at Elinor's insistence, Anna delivers Mary Daniel's baby.

The Bradfords are impervious to the distress of their servants, a number of whom have been with the family for decades. They will not even make the outbuildings available to shelter those who have nowhere to go. Despite their responsibility to their household and, arguably, to the village itself, their primary concern is with themselves. The hypothetical debate of the dinner party several weeks before is now conducted in earnest between Colonel Bradford and

Michael Mompellion. The egotism of the Colonel contrasts with the high-minded altruism of the rector. Yet, interestingly, Mompellion admits that his first instinct was to implore his own wife to leave Eyam. It becomes clear that with privilege comes impunity. Mompellion's prediction that the Bradford name will be 'a hissing in the laneways and the cottages' (p.114) does not come true, and the family's leaving is accompanied by the habitual deference that they have always enjoyed.

Anna herself comes to the unpalatable conclusion that, unlike the Bradfords, she has little choice in the matter. The attitude towards any of the residents of Eyam outside the village is likely to be unwelcoming – a fact that will be validated by the cruel fate of Maggie Cantwell. Anna acknowledges that she will stay because she had 'small will to live – and nowhere else to go' (p.115). While this mindset does not diminish the sacrifice made by the villagers when they agree to the quarantine, the text also illustrates their lack of real choice. Nevertheless, as well as demonstrating the selfishness of the

Bradford family, the crisis also highlights the generosity of others. The homeless servants are taken in by village families and Anna observes that 'as generally happens, those who have most give least, and those with less somehow make shrift to share' (p.117).

Anna embraces the legacy of Anys and Mem, and embarks on the journey which will become her life's work. As Anna prepares to assist Mary Daniel in childbirth, she echoes Anys' chant, invoking her 'grandmothers, the ancient ones' (p.122). Notwithstanding her unwillingness to act as midwife, she deliberately places herself in the tradition of the healing women who have come before her. Her reluctance to deliver the Daniels' baby is based not on indifference, but fear. Anna's own mother died in horrific circumstances that underscore just how dangerous giving birth can be. Elinor, on the other hand, is motivated by practicality – 'we are all she has' (p.121) – and confidence in Anna's ability. Using her 'mother-hands' (p.123), Anna is rewarded with the unexpected blessing of a new life.

Q What is your response to Colonel Bradford's argument?

So soon to be dust

Summary: Maggie Cantwell and Brand are forced back to the village by a frightened and angry crowd in Bakewell; Anna offers to care for Maggie, who has suffered a seizure; Anna has a confrontation with her father; shortly after, Maggie dies.

The violence shown towards Maggie Cantwell and Brand is further evidence of the way in which fear and panic can destroy goodwill. The contrast between the hostility of the Bakewell mob and Brand's own decency is marked: the young man could have left Maggie to her fate, but 'his own goodness drew him back' (p.129). According to Mompellion, the pantry boy becomes the first of the 'heroes' created by the calamity that faces Eyam.

When Anna goes to the Miner's Tavern to organise transportation for Maggie, she encounters her father, drunk and dangerous. His hostile reaction provides a glimpse into Anna's abusive childhood and reinforces the extent of women's vulnerability to men in this society. As the head of his household, it is Bont's prerogative to 'discipline' his wife and children, and both Anna and her mother have been persecuted by this volatile bully. Women are not protected by the law, which does not see fit to intervene in domestic issues. Consequently, women are entirely reliant on the goodwill of the men in their lives. The fact that Anna marries a kind and good husband who is prepared to protect her, simply means that she is luckier than many other women of the time.

In the light of this confrontation, Maggie's subsequent death raises further doubts in Anna's mind. The unfairness of her father being allowed to live 'to waste his reason in drunkenness', while Maggie's 'good and expedient skills' (p.135) die with her, seems insupportable. While Anna caresses Maggie's strong hands, she thinks, as she did with George Viccars and Mem Gowdie, of the expertise that will now be lost and she questions God's 'prodigal' (p.135) response to his creation.

Q What is suggested by Joss Bont's attitude towards the rector?

The poppies of Lethe

Summary: Anna steals some poppy resin from Elinor; she goes to the Gowdies' cottage for more and meets Elinor, who tells Anna her story.

Anna's retrospective voice opens the chapter. She describes her 'Fall', the way in which sin commences with a single wrong step and suddenly 'we are hurtling towards some uncertain stopping point' (p.137). The temptation to resort to the poppy as a way of alleviating the pain that surrounds her is great. Anna, of course, has no idea how addictive the opiate is – she only knows that it once provided the 'sweetest' dreams Sam ever had (p.137) and she simply desires 'a few sweet dreams' of her own (p.138). These dreams seem as remote as they do fantastical, born out of grief and fuelled by yearning. In fact, the white and gold city, 'curving in a wide arc round a sea of sapphire' (p.138), evokes Oran and this luminous prospect, including a family, does await Anna in the future. In the meantime, the death count in Eyam rises by the day. The increasing difficulty of maintaining a sense of purpose and equilibrium in the face of a landscape so dominated by 'utter misery' (p.140) becomes almost too much for Anna to bear. This is Anna's lowest point.

In essence, Elinor saves her. She helps Anna regain her equilibrium by sharing the story of her own past suffering. Elinor shows extraordinary trust in Anna, as well as a finely tuned integrity. She acknowledges that 'I have already asked much of you ... and before this terrible time passes I may ask a great deal more' (p.150). Her honesty and the example she presents invite Anna to look beyond her own pain to consider how she might be of use to others. Elinor's story presents Michael Mompellion in a glowing light; she regards his acceptance of her as generous and selfless. The lifeline he has provided to her is offered, in turn, to Anna. Elinor explains, 'At first, I borrowed his brightness and used it to see my way, and then gradually ... the light in my own mind rekindled itself' (p.155). Anna is rescued by her friend's 'brightness' in exactly the same way. She feels certain that she would 'do anything for this woman' (p.155) and deliberately chooses to lose herself in the work that will benefit the community, rather than in the empty oblivion of the poppy.

Key point

The intimacy between Anna and the rector's wife grows, and Elinor's friendship leads Anna away from the abyss. Together, they will work towards trying to understand how best to combat the plague.

Q Why does Elinor confide in Anna?

Among those that go down to the pit

Summary: *The physical toll on the rector becomes too great; Anna* *persuades her father to dig the graves; Anna and Elinor continue their work, trying to develop health-giving tonics; Anna and Elinor help Merry Wickford to retain her father's mine.*

Mompellion's care for his wretched parishioners is tireless. The sensitivity with which he counsels the dying is particularly evident with Jakob Merrill. Merrill's callous treatment of his deceased wife has weighed heavily on his conscience and, accordingly, he fears his own death. Mompellion allays his anxieties, emphasising the compassion and forgiveness of God towards those who have sinned. However, Mompellion cannot, or will not, extend the same charity to his own wife. The task that Mompellion has set himself in the village becomes too much, even for a man of his formidable strength. Anna enlists the support of her father – for a price – a strategy that will have unexpected and shocking consequences.

The similarities between Michael and Elinor emerge very clearly in this chapter. If Mompellion is indefatigable, so too is Elinor. The determination with which she addresses the twofold challenge of easing the suffering of the afflicted and fortifying the defences of the healthy is ongoing. Gradually, through trial and error, she and Anna build up their store of knowledge. With industry comes some optimism. As Anna chops the efficacious herbs, the rhythmic tattoo of her knife becomes 'the hopeful music of healing' (p.166). Anna is now considered 'part of the rectory family' (p.168), represented by her sharing Elinor's pew in the church.

When Elinor insists that she and Anna go down the Wickford mine, again Anna discovers that she is stronger than she thinks she is. In going underground, she faces the greatest fear left to her, and survives. The pit acts as a metaphor for the crisis engulfing Eyam. Anna's near-death experience of visualising her boys' faces, 'vivid as in life' (p.185), calms her and enables her to accept whatever is forthcoming. Her courage is rewarded and the enterprise secures Merry Wickford renewed hope for the future.

Key point

The strength of Anna's symbiotic partnership with Elinor is one of the 'wonders' to emerge from the plague year. The breakdown of the social order has in fact provided these two women with the opportunity to step outside their circumscribed roles and take initiative in a way that would never otherwise have been possible.

Q How important are traditions in a period of social upheaval?

The body of the mine

Summary: *Joss Bont becomes shamelessly greedy; he is finally called to account by the Barmote Court; as a result of his punishment, he perishes.*

Anna's retrospective voice is very much in evidence throughout the story of her father's reckoning. It is infused with regret and some bitterness: 'all I could think of was the sting of his fist and the stink of his breath' (p.200). Nevertheless, while she deplores his behaviour – now and in the past – she would not have wished such an ending for him. She is also painfully aware of the consequences that lack of intervention brings. Bont's death sets in motion a chain reaction that heaps tragedy upon tragedy.

Bont's conduct demonstrates the most venal (corrupt) response to the crisis presented by the plague. As 'grave-digger to the desperate' (p.190), he brazenly fleeces the villagers for all they are worth. In the past, the community would have taken him to task, but the breakdown of infrastructure enables Bont's wickedness to flourish. Anna witnesses an unexpected side to Mompellion as he remonstrates with her father, countering the latter's abuse with coarse language that 'he did not learn from great Divines at Cambridge' (p.197).

Brooks punctuates the narrative with evocative descriptions of the weather that suggest an imminent reckoning. The sailors' warning implicit in the 'deep rose-red' sky (p.199) and the 'rare spectacle' (p.200) of the advancing storm that whips across the valley foreshadow Bont's fate. Finally, the Barmote Court, 'all that is left of justice in this place' (p.202), intervenes. Although their response is triggered by Bont's attempt to murder Christopher Unwin, their crude judgement is designed solely to protect property and act as a deterrent against theft. As the weather and the plague's malevolence conspire against Bont, he is left to rot. Anna berates herself for not intervening and sadly accepts some responsibility for the 'rage' that comes out of her father's death.

Q Does Anna's refusal to defend her father show strength or weakness?

The press of their ghosts

Summary: The villagers are exploited by Anys Gowdie's 'ghost'; Anna comes to her own conclusions about the plague's origin; the misery caused by the pestilence generates some strange and extreme responses.

Anna grieves for her father and draws on Elinor's support; eventually she is able to balance her 'guilt in the matter of his death' against the debt he owes her 'for the manner of my life' (p.210). However, Bont's death encourages Aphra to continue her own corrupt exploitation of the villagers. The denial of her husband's support – fickle though this may have been – enables her to justify her own behaviour on the basis that she has a child to feed. That she plays on local credulity so successfully shows that the superstitious fears that killed the Gowdies are still widespread.

This chapter focuses on the destructive impact the pestilence has on the township, both emotionally and practically. The loss of tradesmen and farmers creates immeasurable difficulties, and the presence of the dead is so strong that Anna feels their weight as she walks the main street. Fear has a divisive effect, and the villagers now view their neighbours as a danger. Some of the survivors start to behave in bizarre and uncharacteristic ways, as is evidenced by the cases of Jane Martin and John Gordon. To a liberal like Mompellion, Gordon's insistence that the plague is a punishment from God is both offensive and dangerous. Yet Mompellion's own argument that the pestilence has been sent as a test of love becomes increasingly difficult to sustain.

Anna rejects both premises, questioning the whole community's readiness to place the plague in 'unseen hands' (p.214) and reflecting that perhaps an omnipotent God has little to do with the misery that surrounds them. In reasoning that the plague may simply be 'a thing in Nature' (p.215), Anna is voicing a far more serious challenge to prevailing religious doctrine than do the flagellants or other extremist sects.

Key point

Anna concludes that human beings might be better served by acting more proactively to free themselves from pain and illness. This echoes Mem's thinking and places Anna even more squarely in the tradition of modern medical philosophy.

Q What examples do we see in this chapter of Anna's growing assertiveness?

Q Why does she smash the Mompellions' dishes? What does this reveal about her?

A great burning

Summary: *Elinor becomes ill with a fever, but recovers; Mompellion directs the villagers to burn their possessions; Aphra is unmasked as Anys' 'ghost' and punished for her fraud; Aphra slides into madness after the death of her sole surviving child.*

Elinor's illness is confronting to both Anna and Mompellion. In the context of the plague, they each resign themselves to her death. However, Elinor's general flush does not 'blossom into the red-black petals of the Plague's roses' (p.234). Instead, she survives to sit in her beloved garden, surrounded by the 'favourite roses' (p.238) she has grown. This juxtaposition again draws our attention to the polarities of death and survival, and the fragile balance between the two. The jealousy Anna feels towards Mompellion resurfaces during Elinor's illness. There is an implied conflict of interests between the respective possessives of 'her Michael' and 'my Elinor' (p.234). Anna resents Mompellion's presence, and admits to herself that the relationship she shares with Elinor goes far beyond mistress and servant: 'In my own heart, I could whisper it: she was my friend, and I loved her' (p.234).

Mompellion's advocacy of the 'cleansing power of fire' and its use as a 'symbol of rebirth' (p.240) proves to be the village's salvation. Eyam is 'stripped bare' (p.241), metaphorically and physically. As Anna watches the growing pile on the bonfire, she mourns the loss of all those things that cannot be measured, but represent lives shared: 'the unique and private memories of all the many dead' (p.241). The 'great burning' will deliver the village from the scourge of plague, but the skull-like image that Anna sees within the flames also foreshadows the tragedy that will attend deliverance.

Aphra's charms cannot protect her from the rage of the community. In retrospect, Anna can recognise that the villagers are like 'wounded animals, our hurts so raw and our fear so great that we would lash out at anyone' (p.243). At the time, however, it is only the sight of Faith, her small half-sister, that deflects Anna's attention from Aphra. The harsh treatment meted out to her leaves her a 'gibbering, broken thing' (p.246) and the subsequent death of her youngest child tips her over the edge into lunacy. Faith's 'tortured corpse' (p.251) becomes a symbol of all of the impotent victims that have been created by the plague year.

Q What is suggested by Anna's observation that 'Michael Mompellion seemed a man reborn that day' (p.237)?

Deliverance

Summary: *The plague finally abates; as the villagers gather to offer thanks, Elinor is murdered by Aphra.*

The tone of this chapter is elegiac as Anna laments the poignant irony of Elinor's death. Having lived through the plague year, the rector's wife is murdered by Aphra on the very day that the village celebrates its liberation. There is also irony in her presentation as a 'bride', dressed in white, her arms laden with blossoms gathered from her garden, including the ubiquitous 'sprays of fragrant roses' (p.257). Elinor has never been a bride, in the true sense. She has been sacrificed for a principle that, supposedly, ensures her everlasting salvation. Although she and Mompellion have shared a loving relationship, at its core it has been a sham.

Her death is foreshadowed by Anna's reference to a funeral which similarly has flowers and white 'winding sheets' (p.257). Brooks' imagery is very evocative here. Elinor's white gown is violated by the red of a different kind as her blood 'spurting in bright bursts' streaks the dress with crimson, and the scattered flowers receive her 'like a bier' (p.259).

Q Should Anna blame herself over the events leading to Elinor's death?

Leaf-fall, 1666: Apple-picking time

Summary: *Anna has a relationship with Mompellion, but rejects him when he reveals the truth behind his marriage; Anna delivers the Bradford baby and, after saving her life, takes the baby and escapes from Eyam.*

Though the village itself reels on 'in a stunned condition' (p.268), Anna's youth and resilience come to the fore. Her impetuous ride on Anteros is an affirmation of her own miraculous survival: 'I was alive, and I was young, and I would go on until I found some reason for it' (p.273). Riding the horse is also a deliberate challenge to Mompellion's authority and a rejection of the debilitating despair that threatens to swamp them both.

The attraction between Anna and the rector is genuine. However, when Anna discovers the nature of his relationship with Elinor, the abhorrence she feels destroys any possibility of a new beginning with him. Her loyalties lie with Elinor. Mompellion's justification that he acted out of love is overshadowed by his obsession. In fact, love has been used as a weapon: 'The more I could make her love me, the more her penance might weigh in the balance to equal her sin' (p.281). Though she cannot fail to recognise the bitter irony with which he describes himself as 'the husband ... the image of God' casting out 'the whore from Eden' (p.282), she cannot forgive him.

Elinor has paid a heavy price as the result of her seduction. Not only does she initially lose her self-respect and the opportunity to be a mother, her victim status is compounded by her husband's refusal to consummate their marriage. Similarly, Mrs Bradford is grievously punished for her infidelity. She is cast off by the Colonel and forced to relinquish her newborn daughter. However, the birth of this child offers Anna a renewed appreciation of the miracle of existence. The revelation she experiences after delivering the baby directs her to her true calling:

> I knew then that this was how I was meant to go on: away from

death and towards life, from birth to birth, from seed to blossom, living my life among wonders. (p.287)

Q How does Anna 'save' Mompellion?

Epilogue: The waves, like ridges of plough'd land

Summary: Anna sails from England and finally arrives at Oran where she makes a fulfilling new life assisting Ahmed Bey; with her are her two daughters, Aisha and Elinor.

This chapter commences with a reference to women's achievement – a poem by Margaret Cavendish. Anna's new life in the North African city of Oran, 'home of the Andalus Arabs' (p.300), builds on the education and achievement commenced during the plague year. Under the illustrious guidance of Ahmed Bey, Anna's 'craft' has become her 'vocation' (p.300). Avicenna's precious *Canon of Medicine*, which Anna now reads in the original Arabic, not only represents learning and scholarship, but also provides a link between her previous partnership with Elinor and the present.

The occupation that Anna undertakes with the Muslim wives is not only rewarding, but extremely valuable. As she continues to study and learn, she hopes to accomplish 'a worthy life's work here' (p.302). The white and gold city of her dreaming has provided rich opportunity, supportive friends – and a new family. What does the future hold for Anna's two little girls? While the society is strict and women's roles tightly confined, the Muslim culture of Oran is more intellectually liberal and sophisticated than the one that Anna leaves behind.

In choosing Oran as Anna's final resting place, Brooks establishes a connection between *Year of Wonders* and Albert Camus' famous novel, *The Plague*. Camus' bleak and pessimistic novel explores the effect of an outbreak of bubonic plague on the modern city of Oran. Oran becomes a site of struggle and suffering – much like Eyam itself – rather than the city of renewal and promise that Anna finds. The reference to *The Plague* reinforces the ease with which life's pendulum can swing from hope to despair, and back again. However, whereas *The Plague* emphasises the meaningless absurdity of life, *Year of Wonders* celebrates its resilience.

Q What are the differences between Anna's new life and her old one?

CHARACTERS & RELATIONSHIPS

Anna

Key Quotes

'Often, I would stop in the midst of our lessons and laugh for the sheer joy of it.' (p.37)

'I misliked myself for giving way to that fear.' (p.57)

'I hungered for a greater share of her love than I could ever hope for.' (p.229)

'I understood that where Michael Mompellion had been broken by our shared ordeal, in equal measure I had been tempered and made strong.' (p.274)

Anna is an immensely sympathetic protagonist who grows from being, in her own words, a 'timid girl' to 'a woman who had faced more terrors than many warriors' (p.15). Elinor observes the transformation with admiration: 'I wonder if you know how you have changed. It is the one good, perhaps, to come out of this terrible year' (p.235). Elinor recognises her friend's potential from the beginning of their relationship. Anna's thirst for knowledge and genuine love of 'high language' (p.36) has seen her memorise large slabs of the church liturgy. She has even tried to teach herself to read. Under Elinor's tutelage, Anna not only becomes literate, she is also encouraged, sometimes pushed, to test her limits in unprecedented ways. Anna's supple, inquiring mind leads her to ponder, quite early in the text, the polarities of 'dark and light' that define her world (p.55). With the death of her sons, she begins to question the prevailing certainties, and her misgivings continue as the casualties rise. She comes to view God's design as wasteful, and finally asks of the plague: 'Why should this thing be either a test of faith sent by God, or the evil working of the Devil in the world?' Anna's conclusion – that perhaps the scourge 'was neither of God nor the Devil, but simply a thing in Nature' (pp.214–15)

– is fundamentally subversive in its secularism.

Anna's courage has been forged by adversity, and is one of her most obvious and commendable qualities. She has withstood an abusive childhood, early widowhood and the tragic loss of her boys. Throughout the terrible plague year, she has to draw on all of her physical and emotional resources to survive, and there are times when her resolve falters. Yet she quickly becomes one of the most indispensable members of the dwindling community, shouldering the work of the Gowdies and offering ready support to the Mompellions. Like all those with real courage, Anna readily admits to her fears and underestimates her own strength. She turns 'pale' (p.120) at the thought of delivering Mary Daniel's baby, still haunted by memories of her own mother's brutal death in childbirth. Similarly, going underground to mine for Merry Wickford's benefit fills her with terror: 'My cowardice shamed me' (p.183). Nevertheless, she risks her life to assist the child.

By contrast, Anna's refusal to speak for her father is driven by a sense of justice rather than compassion. She is not so magnanimous that she can forgive him, either for his violence towards her as a child or his greed during Eyam's crisis. While she later reproaches herself bitterly for leaving him to his fate, she is able to 'fashion a scale' on which she can weigh her father's nature and 'find a balance between my disgust for him and an understanding of him' (p.210). However, this moral ambivalence is not evident in Anna's defiance of the Bradfords. Her outrage at Elizabeth's attempt to murder the newborn baby is such that Anna physically threatens the woman – a far cry from the automatic deference that characterised their relationship in the past. Anna's passionate commitment to the life that she has just delivered clarifies her future vocation as a midwife: 'I looked into her deep blue eyes and saw reflected there the dawn of my own new life' (p.287).

Anna's love for Elinor underpins much of what she does. She says, after her friend encourages her back from the brink: 'I would try to be the woman that Elinor wished me to be' (p.158). The rector's wife becomes the emotional lynchpin in Anna's life, helping her to overcome despair and reclaim a sense of purpose after the loss of her children. Elinor's example inspires Anna's own heroism and informs many of her actions. Moreover, it is Elinor of whom Anna thinks when she first takes Mompellion in her arms. At times, Anna makes no secret of her jealousy towards Mompellion and his 'greater claim' (p.235) to the place at Elinor's side. The bond between the two women transcends class and social position, and Anna's profound admiration for Elinor generates a fierce, uncritical loyalty. Even Elinor's confession of her past 'sin' cannot diminish Anna's regard for her.

Anna also envies the rector's wife – her grace, her education, her husband. She yearns for the kind of intimacy that she assumes Elinor enjoys in her marriage. The close association between the two women lends a symbolic resonance to Anna's subsequent relations with Mompellion. Anna becomes the surrogate bride, unsuspectingly, though willingly, assuming the role that was Elinor's prerogative. Anna's disgust upon finding out the truth behind the marriage she has so admired fuels her anger, at herself as well as towards Mompellion: 'I had sought to bring her closer to me. I had tried to become her, in every way that I could. Instead ... I had stolen from her' (p.283). The legacy of this emotional triangle continues with the birth of Elinor's namesake. The name Anna gives to her daughter by Mompellion is a significant recognition of Elinor's entitlement to a child, an entitlement that had been taken from her by bitter circumstance. Further, it is a way of celebrating her friend's memory and acknowledging her lasting place in Anna's heart. Nonetheless, Anna comes to understand the importance of emerging from beloved Elinor's shadow and she no longer needs, or wants, to emulate Elinor's literal path. This insight informs the decision to flee England: 'For I was not Elinor, after all, but Anna' (p.299). In fact, she gains an additional identity in Oran – '*Umm*

Jam-ee' (p.303) – that poignantly links her old life with the new.

> ### Key point
> Anna's quest to make sense of the world, her growing skill as a healer and midwife, and her ultimate empowerment are all aspects of her impressive personal journey.

Michael Mompellion

> ### Key Quotes
> 'It was a sermon of love and understanding.' (p.227)
> 'His body is strong, but I fear that the strength of his will far exceeds it.' (Elinor, p.160)
> '...that delicacy masked a most unnatural coldness; that subtle thought had twisted itself into perversion.' (p.284)

Michael Mompellion, the brilliant, charismatic young priest who emerges as the natural leader during Eyam's crisis is not, as Anna naturally assumes, the son of a distinguished family. On the contrary, his career trajectory has been the result solely of personal ability and application and, in fact, demonstrates unusual social mobility for the period. He *has* had the good fortune to attract the attention of a generous patron – Elinor's father – who recognised his academic potential and paid for his education. In marrying Elinor, Mompellion further enhanced his own social standing, though many at the time questioned her decision to marry him.

Mompellion's intelligence and initiative are deployed in the service of Eyam during the plague year. While he assumes leadership reluctantly – mindful of both the Bradfords' natural entitlement and his status in the village as a relative newcomer – it is his vision that ultimately defeats the spread of the contagion. He insists on the quarantine and then develops strategies, such as conducting services in the open air, to minimise the spread. Later, he urges the villagers to burn the flea-infested possessions that carry the 'Plague seeds' (p.227). That he is able to convince the people of Eyam to follow his often unpopular directives says much for his personal commitment and magnetism.

The trauma experienced by Mompellion's own family, following the death of his father, has helped him understand suffering, 'having felt it in his own life' (p.154). He is capable of immense compassion and generosity of spirit. The extent to which he is prepared to support his parishioners, spiritually and physically, throughout the plague year is heroic. He visits the dying, praying with them and writing out their wills, determined to honour his pledge that 'none should die alone' (p.159). He even digs their graves. He continues to push himself, denying himself respite, until he collapses with exhaustion in front of his devastated congregation. In many respects, Mompellion is a man of the people. His humble background and subsequent service on Elinor's family estate have given him a breadth of practical knowledge, as well as an ease in dealing with farmers and tradesmen. He is certainly more than a match for a loutish bully like Joss Bont.

Mompellion's most formidable and most disturbing quality is the strength of his will. Elinor observes, 'It can drive him to do what any normal man cannot do'. Her pensive codicil (addition), 'Believe me, I have seen this, for better and for worse' (p.160), hints at the fact that she, herself, has been the victim of this will. Indeed, nothing more clearly underscores the curious paradoxes that contribute to Mompellion's character than his relationship with his wife. Theologically, Mompellion is a liberal. His relationship with the previous minister, Mr Stanley (officially a 'dissenter'), is inclusive and accommodating. Similarly, his refusal to 'inflame passions on matters that he deemed insignificant' (p.257) is both tactful and pragmatic. He continually preaches the value of forgiveness and deplores the old barbaric punishments of the past. Yet his punishment of Elinor is more painful than the stocks or the cucking stool.

Mompellion's determination to 'save' his wife's soul, whatever the mutual cost, borders on the fanatical, and highlights the dangerous zeal that can accompany religious faith. The Mompellions' marriage has been profoundly compromised by his perverse rationalisation of celibacy as retribution. Moreover, Mompellion's violent response to Jane Martin's drunken wantonness provides a clue to the repressed anger he feels towards Elinor, and perhaps all women.

It is difficult to ignore the phallic connotations behind the name of his horse, Anteros. Mompellion rides a stallion named after the Greek god of requited love. Anteros, the son of Aphrodite and Ares, was deliberately conceived so that his older brother, Eros, could experience love and thus grow to maturity. Anteros was the personification of reciprocal love, as well as the god who punished those who scorned or rejected love. There is a poignant irony here with regard to the Mompellions' situation. The rector does not return love – rather, he rejects its physical expression by refusing to have sexual relations with his wife. The god Anteros was also identified with lust, and some legends have him discharging leaden arrows designed to generate passion without joy. Why Mompellion has chosen to give his horse this name is intriguing. Perhaps it acts as a constant reminder of the dangers and pitfalls of love. Perhaps it is a way of strengthening his resolve and sublimating sexual desire. The timing, therefore, of Mompellion's coupling with Anna is significant, coming as it does immediately after she has set Anteros free from his confinement.

The crisis of faith that Mompellion experiences after his wife's death leaves him a broken man. Not only does his grief and self-loathing overwhelm him, he also rejects the very principle of divine purpose: 'My whole life, all I have done, all I have said, all I have felt, has been based upon a lie' (p.282). He bitterly regrets his intransigence towards Elinor and recognises, too late, the unjustifiable way in which he has punished them both. He even questions his leadership during the plague year and the decision to quarantine the village. Ultimately, Mompellion becomes the symbol of the villagers' loss. Though his judgement *is* vindicated, to many he is perceived simply as 'the bitter emblem and embodiment of their darkest days' (p.269).

Key point

Michael Mompellion's relationship with his wife reveals a more sinister side to his character.

Elinor Mompellion

Key Quotes

'My beautiful friend, full of affection, made for love.' (p.282)

'...as I loved to learn, so she loved to teach.' (p.37)

'The frail body was paired with a sinewy mind, capable of violent enthusiasms and possessed of a driving energy to make and do.' (p.35)

Elinor Mompellion is a remarkable woman – intelligent, compassionate, idealistic, and forgiving. It is her dignity and quiet strength that shine throughout the dark year. Elinor's character gains an added dimension from the painful events of her past – her kindness and reluctance to judge others have been honed by personal suffering. These events have afforded her an insight that may not have been evident had she simply remained protected from the world's malice.

Elinor's background of privilege has given her a graceful confidence in her actions, but this is accompanied by humility rather than ego. Consequently, she cares little for conventional proprieties and is driven solely by concern for others and the dictates of her own conscience. In this regard, she is the antithesis of the proud Bradfords. Elinor is the kind of woman who thinks nothing of engaging a familiar servant in conversation, even as she sits at the table of a wealthy landowner. Equally, when she and Anna take it upon themselves to go down the Wickford mine, it is Anna who fears for her friend's standing in the community: 'I did not rightly know how Elinor Mompellion's reputation would weather this day's doings, falling as they did so far outside what is considered fit for a woman, much less a gentlewoman' (p.187). Elinor herself refuses to be concerned.

Elinor's natural humility has been exacerbated by the 'sin' of her past. Her seduction at 14 and its aftermath have left a permanent legacy of guilt and shame. The burden of it still weighs on her so heavily that she feels it necessary to confide her history to Anna. Rather than seeing herself as the victim that she truly is, Elinor judges herself as harshly as society and her husband have done. Her adult sense of self has been informed by her profound remorse – at dishonouring her family name and destroying the life of her unborn child. Accordingly, she is prepared to accept Mompellion's 'punishment' for her actions. She feels considerable gratitude towards him and views him as her saviour: 'He brought the brightness back into my dim world' (p.154). She insists that, contrary to public perception, 'the sacrifice in the match was all on the side of my dear Michael' (p.155). While the relationship between Elinor and her husband has been overshadowed by the tragedy of her girlhood, there still exists great respect and tenderness between them. Mompellion clearly admires Elinor's determination and demonstrates genuine pride in her achievements.

Elinor's generosity of spirit means that her energies are continually deployed in the service of others. Similarly, once her mind is determined on a course of action, nothing can deflect her. Her influence on Anna is profound. Initially, Elinor acts simply as a mentor. She recognises Anna's potential and takes great pleasure in encouraging her learning. However, Elinor puts the relationship on a more equal and intimate footing when she reveals the details of her past to Anna. Elinor sees it as only fair that Anna truly knows 'who it is that lays these burdens upon you' (p.150). In telling her story – a story that exposes her own vulnerability – she shows considerable trust in the younger woman. In fact, Elinor gains as much as does Anna herself from their relationship. Elinor acknowledges the extent to which she values Anna's friendship when she is ill: 'I am a fortunate woman, to have been loved so in my life' (p.235). It is in this context that Elinor asks Anna to 'be a friend to Mr Mompellion ... For my Michael will have need of a friend' (p.236), an ambiguous request that has more long-lasting implications than either can imagine.

Key point

Elinor refuses to accept the distinctions that her world wishes to make, 'between weak and strong, between women and men, labourer and lord' (p.35).

Josiah (Joss) Bont

Key Quotes

'...my father, in a drunken rage, had flung me against the wall when I was about six years old.' (p.134)

'And then he finally committed an act so vile that even our population, diminished and exhausted, was spurred at last to action.' (p.194)

Joss Bont is one of the villains of the plague year. He views the tragedy merely as an opportunity, and his avarice and insensitivity know no bounds. His ready exploitation of the dying and their families is so blatant that Anna is glad she no longer shares a name with him 'as his became increasingly cursed in every croft and cottage' (p.194). When Bont adds attempted murder to his other crimes, the demoralised village finally calls him to account. Bont's sentence and ignoble death highlight the grievous punishments meted out for crimes against property.

Bont cares nothing for his children and they live in fear of him, just as Anna did as a child. His domestic cruelty is responsible for some of the more nightmarish memories of Anna's early life. She remembers the 'scold's bridle' – an iron cage that was fastened over the head of a woman who offended her husband – and the way in which her mother was led around in it by Bont, 'taunting her, yanking hard on the chain so that the iron sliced her tongue' (p.133). The beatings that Anna endured only ended when she left to marry Sam Frith.

Although Bont has virtually no redeeming qualities, Brooks nevertheless elicits some sympathy for him when the shocking events of his boyhood are revealed. He was a victim of the impressment system – the way in which British merchant ships and the Royal Navy recruited reluctant conscripts throughout the 17th and 18th centuries. Men were effectively kidnapped by 'press gangs' and forced into service at sea where the conditions were harsh and the discipline brutal. As a boy, Bont had been repeatedly raped, whipped and given rum to deaden the pain. All of these abuses have contributed to the man Bont becomes: Anna, and the reader, are at least able to understand what lies behind his depravity and violence.

Aphra Bont

Key Quotes

> 'She was a shrewd woman, my stepmother, in spite of all her superstitious fancies.' (p.107)
>
> 'Aphra enjoyed a pot almost as much as my father, and the two of them spent half their lives in drunken rutting.' (p.40)

Aphra Bont is another character who demonstrates few positive qualities. Yet again, some sympathy is elicited for her, if only because of the fact that she is married to Joss Bont. Aphra is a pragmatic woman whose actions are driven entirely by self-interest, and who seems to have no moral scruples whatsoever. She will not intervene when Bont is beating his eldest daughter and only advises him to stop if he strikes her on the face, for 'we'll never marry her off if you mar her there' (p.134). Like her husband, Aphra exploits the tragedy in Eyam for her own gain, and the plan she devises to rob her desperate neighbours is both ingenious and unscrupulous.

Aphra's case also demonstrates the dangerous ease with which grief can spill over into madness. She is intensely superstitious and is 'ever ready to believe in sky-signs or charms or philtres' (p.39). By the time Aphra has lost all her children to the plague, it is clear that not only is she practising witchcraft, but her reason has left her entirely. In this sense, it is possible to view her as another victim. While Aphra's greed and selfishness deserve condemnation, the crude justice that is meted out to her only serves to fuel her madness and has devastating consequences for others. The final image of the dying Aphra kneeling to kiss her baby's skull, 'with the most exquisite tenderness', is unexpectedly poignant (p.259).

Anys Gowdie

Key Quotes

'She was quick of mind and swift of tongue...' (p.48)

'She was a rare creature, Anys Gowdie, and I had to own that I admired her for listening to her own heart rather than having her life ruled by others' conventions.' (pp.54–5)

Anys Gowdie is an unusual young woman: accomplished, self-reliant and, underneath a proud and sometimes prickly demeanour, remarkably kind – a woman who Anna sadly reflects 'should have been my friend' (p.268). Anys came to live with her aunt Mem as a child of 10, after her own mother died. Anna remembers with admiration the bravado Anys demonstrated when taunted by the local children, who were bemused by her diet of leafy greens. She had retaliated by listing their physical deficiencies, 'standing there taller than any other child her age and glowing with good health' (p.53).

Anys' understanding, from an early age, of the health benefits of various herbs and plants has come from her aunt. Anys and Mem provide Eyam with the 'physick' (medicine) that the villagers need, as well as 'the best chance our women had of living through their confinements with healthy infants in their arms' (p.98). Anys' example, in turn, inspires Anna and it is 'truculent Anys' that Anna hears 'whispering impatiently' in her ear as she tries to deliver the Daniels' baby (p.123). While her manner can be sharp, the sensitive care she shows towards her patients is invariably comforting. For example, when Jamie is dying she effectively soothes his distress with her 'tender and rhythmical' touch (p.84). Similarly, in the birthing room she brings 'a calm kindness' (p.48) to the task that few can match.

Anys' indifference to the opinions of others, or even to the pervasive values of her society, is one of her more interesting qualities. She flatly rejects the idea of marriage, emphasising that her freedom is more important to her than any relationship. Anna is startled at Anys' casual admission that she 'lay with George' and even more at her analogy: 'It was naught more to either of us than a meal to a hungry traveller' (p.53). Yet Anna also respects the other woman, for she understands that 'it takes a kind of courage to care so little for what people whisper' (p.48).

Tragically, Anys becomes the scapegoat for the town's fear and rage. The villagers, spurred on by drink and rage and suspicious of what they do not understand, accuse Anys of witchcraft and blame her for the pestilence. However, Anys remains defiant even as she faces the lynch mob. Rather than plead for her life, Anys goads her tormentors, using their own doubt and superstition as a weapon. Her death, and Mem's shortly afterwards, leaves a terrible absence in Eyam just at the time when the village needs these women the most.

Colonel Bradford

Key Quotes

'Perhaps his military success had made him arrogant, or perhaps such a man should never have retired to the quiet life of a country gentleman.' (p.57)

'I said then, and I say now, that my life and the lives of my family are of more consequence to me than some possible risk to strangers.' (Colonel Bradford, p.112)

Colonel Bradford is the most powerful landowner in the immediate district. During the Civil War he led his men bravely, but in peacetime he demonstrates no such commendable leadership. His household is an unhappy one. Bradford makes no secret of the contempt he feels for his wife, 'a vapid beauty' (p.57) whom he married for her substantial dowry. When Colonel Bradford is in residence at the Hall, his whole family and staff 'tensed like a cur waiting for the boot' (p.58). In this sense, Bradford is not much better than Joss Bont, relying on fear and intimidation to subdue those around him.

When plague is diagnosed in the village, Bradford is driven solely by self-interest. He is ruthless in casting off his servants – many of whom have been with him for decades – and cares little for the fact that they have nowhere else to go. Though his family is 'first' in the area, Bradford refuses to accept that he has a duty to offer support and leadership; rather, he insists that his primary obligation is to his family. It is true that in fleeing the plague, the Bradfords are simply adopting the same strategy as other well-connected families of the time. Nevertheless, the arrogance and ingrained sense of privilege that underpins this decision has even more damning consequences later in the text. When the Colonel's wife gives birth to an illegitimate daughter, his fury at the insult to his family pride is such that he will stop at nothing to rid himself of the child.

Elizabeth Bradford

Key Quotes

'Elizabeth Bradford was a coward. She was the daughter of cowards.' (p.15)

'Even in such a crisis, the woman managed to sneer.' (p.288)

Like her father, Elizabeth holds attitudes and performs actions that are informed by an arrogant sense of privilege. Her condescension towards those whom she deems inferior – such as Anna – is 'overweening' (p.12). Anna dislikes her and, in the past, has deferred to her. However, after the Bradfords' return to the Hall, Elizabeth reveals her vulnerability in front of Anna when she breaks down and blurts out the gravity of her mother's situation.

Elizabeth Bradford is so fearful of her father's fury that she is prepared to murder her newborn half-sister. While she is certainly concerned for her mother, it becomes clear that she also shares Colonel Bradford's determination to protect the family name: 'We cannot have our family's shame flaunted in this village for all to stare at and whisper over' (pp.289–90). Elizabeth's interest in the baby's welfare is negligible, and her willingness to comply with Anna's terms is motivated solely by a desire to be rid of them both as quickly as possible.

THEMES, IDEAS & VALUES

People in crisis

> ### Key Quotes
> 'The Plague is cruel in the same way. Its blows fall and fall again upon raw sorrow, so that before you have mourned one person that you love, another is ill in your arms.' (p.81)
>
> 'Despair is a cavern beneath our feet, and we teeter on its very brink.' (Mompellion, p.256)

Year of Wonders explores the way in which communities respond to crisis, both fearful and heroic. The outbreak of bubonic plague presents the villagers of Eyam with tragedy and dislocation on an unprecedented scale. Over two thirds of the community perishes. This, in turn, creates a breakdown of the social, economic and legal framework that supports the town. Eyam has neither the communal understanding nor the resources to fight the infection, and confusion exacerbates fear. Consequently, the worst responses tend to surface first. Panic and irrationality lead to the ugly lynching of Anys Gowdie. As women who live on the fringe of convention, Anys and Mem are obvious scapegoats; sadly, it is predictable that they will be blamed by a frightened and grieving town. However, in murdering the one and facilitating the death of the other, it is Eyam that also suffers – both in a practical and a moral sense. The text suggests that the greatest threat to a community can come from within and that the damage to the social compact goes beyond the pain inflicted by the plague, terrible though it is.

Fear divides the community and fear 'took each of us differently' (p.218). Some, like Andrew Merrick, withdraw from the village to live a hermit-like existence. Some 'slaked their dread in drink and their loneliness in wanton caresses' (p.218). After losing her whole family, the strict young Puritan woman, Jane Martin, becomes an inebriated bawd who can 'scarce keep her legs closed' (p.218). John Gordon's response is the most extreme. He becomes a flagellant – he stops eating and subjects his body to horrible punishment, scourging himself with plaited leather and nails. In this way, he hopes to purge himself of infection and 'allay God's wrath' (p.221). The majority of the villagers numbly resign themselves to their lack of choice and, in the absence of a caring God, many turn to the superstition that lurks just below the veneer of orthodox religion. Desperate villagers are prepared to pay their last penny for charms and spells against the plague. Kate Talbot expresses the despair of many when she explains to Anna that 'I do not, in my heart, believe in it, and yet I bought this charm because that which I do believe has failed me' (p.145). Sheer fatigue threatens to undo goodwill. The exhausted carter Jon Millstone apologises for his impatience with those who cling to life and therefore require him to harness the cart twice in one day to collect the bodies: 'these times, they do make monsters of us all' (p.141). The times create genuine monsters in the form of the Bonts. Their readiness to exploit the misery of their neighbours provides an extreme example of self-interest over community.

At the same time, the voluntary quarantine of the town is unique, flying in the face of the usual instinct to flee. This selfless decision contains the spread, enabling Mompellion to declare that 'there has been no case of Plague in all of Derbyshire that can be traced to our village' (p.255). The crisis makes 'heroes' (p.130), and creates leaders. The dedicated authority of Michael Mompellion provides a telling contrast to the craven defection of the Bradford family. After the quarantine is implemented, it is the Mompellions and Anna who carry the greatest burden – the rector consoles the dying, while Anna and Elinor support those still living. Their extraordinary commitment to the welfare of the community is indeed heroic. The generosity of individuals such as Brand, the pantry boy from the Hall, is a further reminder of the essential goodness of most people. Crisis also heals division and creates unexpected bonds within the community. The religious differences pale in comparison to the common danger that attacks Anglican and dissenter alike. Anna is heartened by the hesitant attendance of the nonconformists at the Sunday services. It is a further 'wonder' that emerges from tragedy (p.168). Many maintain their faith, despite the way in which it is tested.

The town's plight is set against a broader social context. In many respects, Eyam may be regarded as a microcosm, a reflection of the wider world, which exemplifies the way in which communities respond to crisis. The account of the Bradfords' London guest paints a grim picture of ruthlessness and misery. The dying are locked alone in their houses, marked with the menacing red crosses as communal self-interest again comes to the fore. Like Eyam, London produces its heroes as well as its cowards – while the majority who can choose to flee, some, like Lord Radisson, argue that it is their duty to stay and provide an 'example' (p.61) to those less fortunate.

The strength of women

Key Quotes

'…in many ways, the well-being of our village rested more on her works, and those of her aunt, than on the works of the rectory's occupant.' (p.55)

'I think you like to go and come without a man's say-so.' (Anys, p.54)

In the 17th century, women were 'shackled to their menfolk as surely as the plough-horse to the shares' (p.55). Society's gender expectations were narrow and proscribed, and the opportunities presented to women were extremely limited. In general, their roles were confined to the domestic. Yet there is a strong feminist consciousness operating throughout *Year of Wonders*. History books have habitually suppressed the female voice, but novels such as this attempt to redress that balance.

Brooks alludes to the powerful support network that women have traditionally established for themselves and their communities. The Gowdies are strong, independent women who play an invaluable role in the life of the village. Mem and her niece, Anys, are part of a tradition of wise women who tend the physic garden from which they make their efficacious brews. This garden is very old and they see themselves merely as its custodians: 'My aunt and I are just the latest in a long line of women who have been charged with its care' (p.51). Anys' comment is a reminder of the way in which homeopathic knowledge has been shared and passed down through the generations. The Gowdies' midwifery skill is another indispensable aspect of their service to Eyam. Women's particular vulnerability in childbirth is graphically illustrated in the text, and it is the Gowdies' expertise that has often made the difference between life and death. They provide a very different alternative to the brutal and invasive methods of the barber-surgeons. Furthermore, as committed healers, the Gowdies are unstinting in their assistance towards those in need – again, a marked contrast to the surgeons who 'would not stir without the clank of shillings to line their pockets' (p.74).

Nevertheless, the village's dependence on the Gowdies' services is offset by the inevitable suspicion that their knowledge and self-sufficiency incite. There is a delicate and uneasy equilibrium that must be maintained: 'I knew how easy it is for widow to be turned witch in the common mind' (p.38). This balance is destroyed when the plague strikes Eyam.

The Gowdies represent a challenge to the values of the period in several ways. First, they are single women living alone without the protection of men, or the necessity to defer to them. Second, their medicinal learning sets them apart from the other villagers who tend to be driven by blind faith or superstition, or a combination of the two. Third, both Mem and Anys are intelligent women who think outside the prevailing norm. For example, Mem does not believe that illness is a foregone conclusion predetermined by God and argues that individual intervention can make a difference. This, of course, directly contradicts the minister's, Mr Stanley's, view that human beings have no right to evade 'the lessons God willed us to learn' (p.39). Mem's niece, Anys, is even more unconventional. She has no aspirations to marry – 'I'm not made to be any man's chattel' (p.54) – and chooses her sexual partners as the mood takes her. Her real fulfilment comes from her work. She explains to Anna that 'I have something very few women can claim: my freedom. I will not lightly surrender it' (p.54). However, Anys' proud independence has generated criticism, as well as envy, and there are many who whisper maliciously behind her back. Perversely, Anys' authority lives on after her brutal murder. Aphra is able to exploit the villagers' awe of Anys' healing powers when it becomes clear that desperate and foolish people are still prepared to pay for advice from her 'ghost'.

After the Gowdies' deaths, it is left to Anna to preserve their legacy and continue their work. It is she who is marked as next in the 'long line of women', though her calling as a healer eventually takes her to an exotic destiny far from England. The physical and emotional toll demanded of Anna during the plague year is great. The loss of her sons nearly breaks her and she is tempted to seek oblivion in the poppy. Yet Elinor's gentle example and the solace of work provide a reason to continue. Anna emerges from the crisis wiser and more self-assured than before. She grows from a simple, uneducated village girl to a formidable woman who is even capable of defying the mighty Bradfords. In the interview included at the end of the novel, Brooks talks about the inspiration behind Anna's character. The remarkable strength demonstrated by women in the war zones of the Middle East and Africa underscores the way in which adversity creates heroines, albeit unlikely ones: 'These women would suddenly find themselves having to step out of their old roles and assume vastly challenging responsibilities' (p.317). The same can be said for both Anna and Elinor. Brooks suggests that, whatever the context, women are more than capable of responding with courage and resourcefulness, despite conventional limitations imposed by gender and upbringing. Like the modern women cited by Brooks, Elinor and Anna step out of the roles that history has assigned to them to proactively support their community. Perhaps the most telling example in the text of women repudiating the 'feminine' role is when Anna and Elinor go down the Wickford mine. While it is Elinor who initiates this rather rash scheme, Anna is the one who facilitates its successful outcome.

Key point

The social upheaval generated by the onset of plague actually provides women with opportunities to lead and exercise initiative in a way that has previously been denied to them.

Loss and survival

Key Quotes

'These memories of happiness are fleeting things, reflections in a stream, glimpsed all broken for a second and

> then swept away in the current of grief that is our life now.' (p.6)
> 'And, for an hour, in that season of death, we celebrated a life.' (p.125)

By June 1666, Eyam has buried half of its citizens. Anna herself has had to survive the worst that a mother can endure when her two young children are taken from her. Whole families in the town are struck down, houses stand empty, and starving animals wander untended. Anna senses the presence of the dead, even as she mourns their loss: 'Sometimes, if I walked the main street of the village in the evening, I felt the press of their ghosts' (p.217). The practicalities of the death toll run in tandem with the grief of losing friends and neighbours, and functioning without skilled tradesmen becomes yet another burden to be shouldered. Eyam seems cut off from the rest of humanity and, increasingly, isolated from God.

Loss of faith is a further casualty as it becomes more and more difficult to sustain belief in the Divine in the face of such devastation. Brooks explores the impact on a close-knit community when faith is shattered. The vacuum that is created provokes a range of responses – anger, disorientation, despair – and some of these reactions incite further misery. Anna is not the only one to question the dreadful way in which Eyam is tested. Ironically, Michael Mompellion, whose certainty and sense of purpose has kept the village going throughout the plague year, loses that faith when his own wife dies. Beside himself with grief and remorse, he rebuffs all attempts at comfort – from Anna and also, significantly, from Mr Stanley. He categorically rejects the latter's message of acceptance – a message that he himself would have preached in times gone by. Anna observes helplessly that 'It was as if he commenced upon a journey at the moment of Elinor's death, and every day he moved farther and farther away, seeking for some refuge in the recesses of his own mind' (p.264).

Yet despite being a novel about loss and death, *Year of Wonders* celebrates life. Miraculously, Eyam *does* survive as a community. Once the threat of plague subsides, notwithstanding the horrific losses and the profound damage to morale, there are glimmers of a more positive future. Neighbours form new bonds, tentative friendships develop – such as the one between Merry Wickford and Jane Martin – and these relationships have a healing effect. Anna acknowledges that 'life is not nothing, even to the grieving. Surely humankind has been fashioned so, otherwise how would we go on?' (p.255). Anna's own role as a healer and midwife, by definition, reinforces the intrinsic value of 'going on', and the moments of affirmation provided by the onset of new life counterbalance the relentless suffering in the text.

The text argues strongly that the will to survive comes from the crucial encouragement of the living. Grief and loss can be assuaged by the support of others who help reinvigorate a sense of purpose. Personal salvation comes from example and service. There is a clear pattern in the way in which the three main characters are 'saved' by each other. Elinor's deliverance comes when Mompellion rescues her from opium-induced depression. She provides similar guidance and incentive to Anna when the latter needs it most. Anna, in turn, recalls Mompellion to his duty when he is immersed in the mire of his own distress. He admits with gratitude that 'you have saved more than two lives this day' (p.293). Interestingly, both Anna and Mompellion shift from the conventional belief that faith in God is necessary to lead a good and purposeful life, to a position of relative agnosticism. Mompellion's conclusion – 'One does not have to believe, after all, to bring comfort to those who yet do' (p.293) – is comparable to the outlook Anna expresses in Oran.

The prophetic consolation Anys offers to Anna when she loses her children reinforces the idea that life can offer unexpected gifts as well as overwhelming tragedy. Anna *does* become a mother again and the joy of having her daughters offsets trauma with hope, emptiness with love. The name that Anna gives her elder daughter – Aisha, meaning bread or life – is apposite (appropriate), 'for she sustained me' (p.303). The ending of the text is a validation of life's rich possibility, as well as being a testimony to the optimism implicit in new beginnings.

Religious faith versus knowledge

> ### Key Quotes
> 'So where, exactly, in the design of the world, did I believe that matters tilted the scale sufficient to garner God's notice?' (p.215)
> 'Untrue in one thing, untrue in everything.' (p.267)

At the heart of the novel is the conflict between emerging knowledge – scientific and medicinal – and religious faith. In Anna's world, all things are measured against a spiritual rather than a temporal yardstick. The common Christian belief – whether Puritan or papist – is that God determines the affairs of humanity. Furthermore, the religious intensity that characterises the period often tips over into superstition. Most people believe in the Devil as passionately as they believe in God – indeed, the two go hand in hand. Anna has been taught to view the world in terms of polarities: 'The Puritans who had ministered to us here had held that all actions and thoughts could be only one of two natures: godly and right, or Satanic and evil' (p.55). The plague, therefore, must be either a divine response to a sinful world or satanic malice against the god-fearing. Any suggestion otherwise is considered presumptuous. Those who do argue that the scourge might not be supernaturally prompted, such as the Gowdies, are rendered vulnerable by their lack of orthodoxy.

Anna also challenges this prevailing view when she hypothesises that 'If we balanced the time we spent contemplating God, and why He afflicted us, with more thought as to how the Plague spread and poisoned our blood, then we might come nearer to saving our lives' (p.215). Her supposition implies that, first, too much time has been wasted in religious speculation to the detriment of more rational thinking and, second, that human beings actually have the intellectual capacity to function independently, without divine intervention. Indeed we *should* do so. In rejecting the idea of 'some grand celestial design' (p.215), Anna is mounting the modern argument for self-determinism. If it were possible to find 'the tools and the method and the resolve' (p.215), Eyam could free itself, 'no matter if we were a village full of sinners or a host of saints' (p.215). In concluding that faith is irrelevant to any given outcome, Anna's own loss of faith follows logically. In this, she pre-empts the thinking of many in the contemporary world.

Key point

Crisis facilitates a change in thinking and encourages individuals to re-examine existing beliefs.

Sacrifice

Key Quotes

'Let the boundaries of this village become our whole world. Let none

> enter and none leave while this Plague lasts.' (Mompellion, p.104)
>
> 'And yet the current times did seem to ask us all for every kind of sacrifice...' (p.173)

The quarantine of the people of Eyam is the most striking example of sacrifice in the text. The Sunday Oath is taken in a spirit of altruism and binds the villagers as hostages for as long as the pestilence rages. The clear intention is to protect the wider world from plague. In electing to stay in their 'wide green prison', the villagers act in the selfless knowledge that they increase their own chances of contracting the disease.

Mompellion's success in persuading the town to accept the quarantine is, of course, a testament to his personal commitment and charisma. Nevertheless, the compliance of the villagers is also a corollary of the ingrained deference towards their superiors that has been instilled from birth. They automatically look to a higher authority – the rector, if not the Bradfords – to provide direction, even resolution. Furthermore, the concept of sacrifice is a familiar one to this devout community. Their understanding of the surrender of self is informed by Christian ideology and Mompellion draws on this deeply embedded value in his compelling argument for the quarantine. He refers to the example of Christ's sacrifice, and the love which motivated it, encouraging the townspeople to follow suit: 'Were we not bound to return this love to our fellow humans?' (p.101). In accepting the 'Cross' (p.104) offered, two-thirds of the villagers sign their death warrants. Anna sadly wonders if future generations will remember the 'great sacrifice that we made here' (p.274).

The explicit correlation between sacrifice and love is also played out on a personal level. Sacrifice underpins the Mompellions' marriage. Elinor believes that Michael has sacrificed himself in marrying her, but she is the true sacrifice. Though Elinor accedes to Mompellion's terms out of guilt, the platonic nature of their marriage clearly causes her pain, as is evidenced by her delirious pleading when she is ill.

Mompellion's refusal to consummate the relationship evokes the image of a traditional sacrificial lamb. Elinor's temporal happiness and sexual fulfilment are used by her husband as a bargaining chip, sacrificed to avert the retribution of an offended God. Mompellion contends that this is the only way Elinor can expiate her 'troubled soul' (p.280), thus guaranteeing her spiritual salvation.

Mompellion's final sermon in the village church offers a clue as to his dogmatism on this issue. He argues, 'Who but a negligent father allows his children to grow up unguided by sometime chastisements?' (p.168). At the same time, a good father 'deals the necessary penances with love in his eyes' (p.168). Mompellion's paternalism towards his wife is both cultural and religious. He has convinced himself that the sacrifice will save her soul and believes that it is his duty to implement it. In his mind, there is a clear distinction between repentance and atonement: 'My Elinor I *had* to be assured was cleansed' (p.281). Anna oversimplifies Mompellion's position when she rejects it as vindictive. The pact that the couple made is difficult for them both and Mompellion is punishing himself as well as Elinor: 'For of course I did love her and desired her, no matter how hard I turned the press down upon my own feelings' (p.282). While there is certainly evidence of some repressed anger on Mompellion's part, there is also love – however misguided.

At the end, Mompellion's disillusionment is such that the two issues – the sacrifice of the town and the sacrifice that he demands of Elinor – have become blurred in his own mind. Legitimate guilt and recrimination over the latter invite him to reject the former as equally arrogant and misguided. His self-doubt is so strong at this point that he questions all his past actions. Nevertheless, the decision to quarantine Eyam is undeniably in the best interests of the wider community, and is in line with modern practice.

DIFFERENT INTERPRETATIONS

Different interpretations arise from different responses to a text. Over time, a text will give rise to a wide range of responses from its readers, who may come from various social or cultural groups and live in very different places and historical periods. These responses can be published in newspapers, journals and books by critics and reviewers, or they can be expressed in discussions among readers in the media, classrooms, book groups and so on. While there is no single correct reading or interpretation of a text, it is important to understand that an interpretation is more than a personal opinion – it is the justification of a point of view on the text. To present an interpretation of the text based on your point of view, you must use a logical argument and support it with relevant evidence from the text.

Critical viewpoints

The critical reception that *Year of Wonders* received when it was first published was largely favourable. Reviewers have generally been united in their praise of the novel. Eyam's tribulations have been viewed as an inspiring study of a community in crisis which also has some resonance for our own times. Alfred Hickling, writing for *The Guardian,* called it 'a tale of fragile hope pitted against overwhelming disaster'. The authenticity of the historical voice and the lyricism of the writing have been consistently cited as strengths. Similarly, Brooks' 'multi-layered and expressive characterisations' (Thompson 2002) that, even in the worst instances, still elicit some sympathy have been commended as adding complexity to the narrative.

Nevertheless, there have been a few 'caveats'. Kathy Weissman (2009) argued that the text suffers from too 'modern' an agenda. For Weissman, Anna's religious speculation and independence of thought verge on the 'too-good-to-be-true', while Anys and

Mem are implausibly aberrant. Weissman suggested that Brooks goes too far 'in making 17th century women into modern ones'. There have also been some concerns expressed about the resolution of Anna's story. Descriptions of the ending range from a 'delicious' surprise (Weissman 2009) to an 'adventure' that compromises the unity of the novel, 'challenging credulity beyond measure' (Corbett 2005), to 'border-line risible' (Kirkus Reviews 2006). The diversity of these views points to the different ways in which readers can interpret elements of any given text.

Two possible interpretations

Reading 1

Year of Wonders suggests that a strong religious belief system, however flawed, adds to a society's wellbeing and happiness.

In the 17th century, religion played a central role in the lives of the people. While *Year of Wonders* does not present religious belief, or those who espouse it, as without fault, the text illustrates how positive a force a strong belief system can be. Religious faith provides individuals with the incentive and inspiration to work selflessly for the benefit of their societies. This is particularly apparent in a time of crisis or adversity.

The church is the centre of community life in Eyam, with the rector and his wife playing significant roles. In the absence of any system of social service, it is the Church of England ministry that provides material support, as well as spiritual guidance. In this capacity, Michael and Elinor Mompellion are both presented as forces for good in the life of the village. Mompellion's arrival in the town does much to defuse religious tension. In comparison to the previous incumbent, Mr Stanley, the younger priest's version of the Christian message is inclusive and tolerant. He is sensitive to Mr Stanley's political ostracism and encourages him to return to 'the place and people he best knew' (p.100). Nor is Mompellion prepared to endorse the harsh laws with regard to nonconformist 'meetings'. Elinor's mission of communal service is born out of her Christian faith and the list of her charities is extensive. She concerns herself with every aspect of village life – visiting the sick and elderly, counselling the troubled, mothering the neglected, and 'making herself indispensable in any number of ways to all kinds and classes of people' (p.38).

This selfless commitment to community is evident when disaster strikes. The Mompellions' faith instils a clear sense of duty and enables them to act with great altruism. Had it not been for the Mompellions, the villagers – most of whom are not in a position to leave Eyam – would have been bereft of moral guidance or practical leadership. Mompellion's management of the crisis is decisive and effective. Having initiated the quarantine, he organises the logistics of Eyam's 'voluntary besiegement' (p.104) and offers unqualified support to his parishioners. Similarly, Elinor's willing collaboration provides ongoing assistance to those in need. The weekly church service becomes the one reassuring constant during a period of unprecedented trauma and, encouraged by Mompellion's generous example, the community is sustained by its earnest belief in God's mercy. Mompellion persuades his congregation to draw on its faith – 'Beloved, do not lose sight ... of God's great love and tenderness' (p.168). The rector pledges that 'while I am spared no one in this village will face their death alone' (p.106) and his ministry to the dying highlights the consolation afforded by religious belief.

The text primarily focuses on the positive impact of a strong belief system within a Christian context. However, the value of religious belief is also demonstrated through the character of Ahmed Bey. Faith – the 'adamantine one by which the doctor measures every moment of his day' (p.301) – underpins the physician's service to his community. He interprets Anna's arrival as Allah's 'pity on a tired old man' (p.301) and is therefore prepared to take her on as his assistant, despite the unconventional nature of her presence in his household.

Year of Wonders demonstrates how a strong religious belief system provides a structure within which individuals act generously and unselfishly for the betterment of their communities. The spiritual comfort offered by religious faith, particularly in a time of crisis, is further evidence of the way in which such a belief system contributes to a society's general wellbeing and peace of mind.

Reading 2

Year of Wonders is highly critical of the role religion plays in the life of 17th-century society.

Year of Wonders examines the destructive impact of religion in the 17th century. The text argues strongly that, in terms of both the individual and society itself, religion is a negative force. The context within which the novel is set is presented as religiously divisive, and tensions between Christian factions still undermine the equilibrium of society. Puritans are 'few among us now, and sorely pressed' (p.7). Quaker families like the Wickfords have been actively persecuted, victims of the bigotry bred by religious intolerance.

Eyam itself is a devout community. However, in the face of the devastation wrought by the plague it becomes difficult to retain religious faith. The early trust of the villagers is depicted as naive and misguided: 'At that time, you see, we all of us believed that God listened to such prayers' (p.95). Despite the insistence of their clergy, the people come to feel they are praying in a void – God is not listening and does not appear to care. Anna's personal disillusionment is shared by many: 'After so many unanswered prayers, I had lost the means to pray' (p.290). Yet the villagers cannot relinquish the deep-seated belief that the supernatural wields power over their lives. In their desperation, they turn to superstition, often with disastrous results. Faith in God is replaced, in some instances, with faith in the Devil. Aphra Bont is able to capitalise on this susceptibility – she also becomes a victim of it.

Religion is shown to breed extremism as the line between faith and obsession becomes very blurred. With regard to John Gordon, Elinor explains to Anna that flagellants 'have ever been the spectre that stalks with the Plague' (p.220). While Mompellion recognises the dangers fanaticism begets and is determined to root it out, ironically he fails to perceive the parallels between Gordon's situation and his own. When Urith Gordon describes the mortifications that her husband insists they both practise, and confides that they are not 'to take any comfort of each other's bodies, but lie always chaste' (p.225), there are uncomfortable echoes of the Mompellions' marriage. The description of the rector's voice evokes the same stark polarities of 'light and dark' (p.45) that define the 17th-century world and reflects Mompellion's rigid interpretation of God's message as it applies to his wife. Furthermore, while Mompellion's commitment to his ministry is commendable, the text suggests it is an aberration. Few of his fellow Anglican priests seem to share his loyalty to their congregations and are quick to flee the danger presented by the plague.

Finally, religion is presented as discouraging freedom of thought and, in this sense, it impedes intellectual progress. The stranglehold that religious belief exerts over the majority stifles debate and initiative. Religious rationale with regard to the plague ranges from the conventional perception that it is a punishment from God to Mompellion's claim that it is an opportunity to emulate Christ's example. Mr Stanley insists that the apparently random nature of the disease is because 'God bestows suffering on those whom He would spare from torments after death' (p.232). However, the religious perspective never questions the principle of divine responsibility, and the idea that individuals may hold the answer in their own hands is considered blasphemous. Accordingly, the societal response tends to be either passive or reactive. There are few in the West who are proactively trying to solve the medical mystery.

Although the text acknowledges the fundamental importance of religion in the lives of the people at this time, it is also highly critical of its pervasive authority. Overall, religious belief is depicted in a negative light.

QUESTIONS & ANSWERS

Essay topics

1 Michael Mompellion tells Anna that he was "most shockingly wrong, in what I asked of this village". Do you agree?
2 *Year of Wonders* shows just how little real power individuals have.' Discuss.
3 "This Plague will make heroes of us all, whether we will or no." How heroic are the people of Eyam?
4 *Year of Wonders* suggests that, in a time of crisis, it is more important than ever to hold on to traditional values.' Discuss.
5 "I wonder if you know how you have changed." What has caused the changes in Anna?
6 *Year of Wonders* demonstrates the destructive power of love.' Discuss.
7 'This text demonstrates the difficulties of holding on to faith in times of adversity.' Discuss.

8 'Michael Mompellion's powerful need for control is behind many of his actions.' Do you agree?

9 'The women in *Year of Wonders* are stronger than the men.' Do you agree?

10 "...choices no longer had that same clear, bright edge to them." Does Anna always choose wisely?

Vocabulary for writing on Year of Wonders

Allegory: a story with a meaning or message other than the literal one – the text invites interpretation on at least two levels.

Bubonic plague: deadly pandemic that swept through Europe from the 14th to the 17th centuries.

Circular structure: the narrative begins and ends at the same, or a similar, point.

First-person narration: the story is told in the first person from the perspective of one of the main characters.

Historical fiction: the genre to which *Year of Wonders* belongs – draws on events from the past as the basis for a work of fiction.

Motif: a recurring image used to link ideas and reinforce themes – adds cohesion and unity to the writing.

Papist: Roman Catholic.

Patriarchy: a society where all the power structures – political, religious, legal and domestic – are invested in men.

Puritan: Protestant who promotes a stricter, 'purer' form of Christianity.

Retrospective narrative: the protagonist of a text looks back retrospectively on past events – affords them the added advantage of hindsight and invites reflection on previous experiences.

Romance: a narrative that explores a romantic relationship between individuals.

The Restoration: the period in English history (1660–85) in which the text is set – alludes to the restoration of Charles II to the throne.

Analysing a sample topic

'...choices no longer had that same clear, bright edge to them.' Does Anna always choose wisely?

This question focuses on the character of Anna and invites you to evaluate the choices that she makes. You are asked a direct question here – you must answer it! Make your contention clear in the introduction and indicate your line of argument.

- What are Anna's choices? Identify those that are particularly important and affect her growth as an individual.
- Key words: 'always', 'wisely'. Is it possible *always* to choose wisely? Is it imperative that people do so? The underlying assumption here is that wise is preferable, but does the text always reinforce this? For example, Anna's choice to deploy 'fire and water' in order to free the ore from the Wickford mine is foolhardy – but brave, and ultimately effective.
- Consider the context in which the topic quotation appears. What does

this suggest about the decisions people make?
- Examine Anna's motivation. Why does she behave in the way she does? Look objectively at Anna's actions, rather than merely accepting what she says at face value.
- What are the consequences of Anna's decisions? Who or what benefits? Is anybody hurt by the choices she makes?

The following plan is *one* way to tackle the topic, though the weight of evidence in the text *does* suggest that Anna's choices are worthwhile.

Sample introduction

>Year of Wonders by Geraldine Brooks charts Anna's journey to independence and fulfilment. As Anna deliberates over George Viccars' offer of marriage, she acknowledges that life's options are not always black and white, but composed of various shades of grey. With the growing wisdom that accompanies maturity, she can observe that it is not always easy

to make prudent decisions. In this case, for example, she must consider the welfare of her sons as well as her own desires. While Anna herself is sometimes critical of her own actions, she does generally choose wisely. In this, she is guided by her 'superior' intelligence, a finely honed conscience, and unswerving courage.

Paragraph outline

Paragraph 1: Anna's choice to follow Elinor's lead and actively respond to Eyam's 'agonies' benefits both herself and her community.
- Anna is tempted to escape in the 'empty' oblivion of the poppy after the deaths of her sons.
- However, she chooses instead to 'lose' herself in 'the study and its applications' that will help fight the plague.
- Her friendship with Elinor is the catalyst that inspires action.
- She develops medicinal expertise and midwifery skills → takes up the Gowdies' mantle.

Paragraph 2: Though many of Anna's actions are intuitive rather than premeditated, they are no less worthwhile for that.
- Anna's rejection of Mompellion is in *both* their interests – relationship would have been conducted in the shadow of Elinor's memory.
- Her impulsive decision to take Aisha offers new hope: 'To have saved this small, singular one – this alone seemed reason enough that I lived.'
- Resolution to leave England and disembark in Oran – follows her vocational instinct → provides a new life for herself and her daughters.

Paragraph 3: While Anna is critical of some of her own actions, she cannot be held responsible for the way in which events play themselves out.
- She chooses not to defend her father – a formality that was unlikely to have made any difference to his sentencing.
- Feels guilty for not rescuing her father, but believes Aphra will do it: 'It never occurred to me that she would not.'

- Similarly, no way of knowing that Aphra's madness will wreak such havoc.
- Only with the value of hindsight can Anna see the tragic pattern that unfolds.

Sample conclusion

Year of Wonders examines the choices that confront Anna throughout the course of a profoundly difficult year. Elinor Mompellion admires the fact that Anna has become a confident woman of great skill and understanding from 'such scant stuffs' that her life initially provided. Anna's metamorphosis is partially born out of the perceptive choices that she makes – these changes also inform further decisions. The qualities that Anna persistently demonstrates – courage, integrity and insight – enable her to strike a balance between remaining true to herself and making judgements that are in the best interests of those around her. In terms of the important milestones that mark her personal journey, Anna *does* choose wisely.

SAMPLE ANSWER

'*Year of Wonders* shows just how little real power individuals have.' Discuss.

Geraldine Brooks' compelling historical novel *Year of Wonders* explores the way in which people's lives can be overtaken by unforeseen tragedy. The onset of bubonic plague in the English village of Eyam creates enormous suffering and destroys the social fabric of the community. Most of the population has little power in relation to its fate. In addition, the broader social context of the 17th century imposes its own limitations. Class, gender and cultural expectations all exert a crucial influence on the way individual lives are played out. Nevertheless, while circumstances may be beyond individual control, the choice to behave with integrity and dignity remains. The text demonstrates that it is possible for some strong, courageous characters to exercise initiative and assume control over their personal destinies.

In a rigid, class-orientated society, 'wealth and connection are no shield against Plague'. The lack of understanding in relation to the plague means that there are few strategies with which to fight it. There is no cure or antidote. Nor does the 'contagion' discriminate between rich and poor, and the apparently arbitrary nature of the spread compounds the general panic. Yet, inevitably, it is the poor who are the most vulnerable. The option to escape infected neighbourhoods is denied to them as travel necessitates funds and an alternative destination. Furthermore, any person travelling from a plague-affected area is regarded as a social pariah. The violence directed towards Maggie Cantwell and Brand, when they try to flee Eyam, is presented as endemic. The young Londoner tells of the 'angry mob' he encountered, 'brandishing hoes and pitchforks, denying entry to their village to any who were travelling from London'. The possibility that an individual may carry the 'plague seeds' guarantees the hostility and intolerance of the outside world. It is only wealthy families like the Bradfords who are insulated by their privileged status.

Choices in the 17th century are predetermined by gender, as well as social position. The novel highlights how little true power women possess, relative to men. Moreover, privilege alone does not necessarily assure protection. Mrs Bradford, for example, is trapped in an abusive marriage with a husband who 'has ever been cruel to her'. When she becomes pregnant with another man's child, Bradford 'excels himself in his wretchedness'. Mrs Bradford is not only rejected by the Colonel – he also denies his wife medical support during her labour, essentially leaving her to die. It becomes clear to Anna that the surgeon must have been 'under instructions to be negligent'. Mrs Bradford is forced to give up her baby and can only thank Anna for her timely intervention: 'Tell her that her mother would have loved her, if she had been allowed'.

However, the text also illustrates the way in which individuals can empower themselves. Eyam's remarkable story is a testimony to the way in which a small community can make a significant difference to the wider world. While the options open to the villagers may be limited in real terms, the fact that they voluntarily choose to instigate a quarantine is a resolute declaration of self-determination. Mompellion persuades his congregation to recognise the dangerous power that can transport the disease further afield: 'Let the boundaries of this village become our whole world'. The unselfish swearing of the Sunday Oath protects the surrounding countryside from 'proximity to the ill', thus containing the spread of plague.

Equally, some individuals are able to assert control over their own lives. Despite her gender and her poverty, Anna is empowered by a number of critical decisions that affect not only her future, but also the lives of others. Her rejection of a relationship with Mompellion, coupled with her spontaneous offer to take the Bradford baby, reconciles Mompellion to his 'duties'. He credits Anna with rescuing him by her example: 'I do not propose to go on as I have been, feeding on the gall of my own grief'. Clearly, her intercession also saves the child's life. Rather than accepting Mompellion's advice to seek refuge with his old patron, Anna bravely chooses to leave England. In severing 'every tie that bound me to my old life', she emancipates herself from the legacy of the previous year and finds new direction in the Arab world for herself and her daughters.

In conclusion, it is sadly evident that most individuals in *Year of Wonders* have little real power. The plague is a horrific leveller, targeting rich and poor alike, and devastating everything in its path. The lack of knowledge and effective resources means that the majority must resign themselves to a miserable fate. Individuals are further constrained by societal factors such as poverty and gender. At the same time, there *are* characters in the novel whose courage and enterprise encourage them to exercise some autonomy, even to the extent of shaping events and influencing outcomes.

REFERENCES & READING

Text

Brooks, Geraldine 2001, *Year of Wonders,* HarperCollins, London.

Books

Camus, Albert 1948, *The Plague,* Penguin Books, Harmondsworth.

Miller, Arthur 2000, *The Crucible,* Penguin, London.

Film

Restoration 1995, dir. Michael Hoffman, Miramax Films. Starring Robert Downey Jr and Sam Neill.

Websites

Brooks, Geraldine 2009, *Geraldine Brooks,* www.geraldinebrooks.com/

Corbett, Bob 2005, *Year of Wonders,* www.webster.edu/~corbetre/personal/reading/brooks-year.html

Hickling, Alfred 2001, *Journal of a plague year,* www.guardian.co.uk/books/2001/jul/14/fiction.reviews

Kirkus Reviews 2006, *Year of Wonders: A Novel of the Plague,* LitLovers, www.litlovers.com/guide_yearwonders.html

Thompson, William 2002, *Year of Wonders: A Novel of the Plague,* SF Site Reviews, www.sfsite.com/06b/yw130.htm

Weissman, Kathy 2009, *Year of Wonders,* Bookreporter.com, www.bookreporter.com/reviews/0142001430.asp

Wikipedia 2009, *Anteros, Derbyshire lead mining, The Great Plague of London,* en.wikipedia.org

For more Insight English resources, including over 100 text guides on classic and contemporary literature and film, as well as complete school editions of Shakespeare's most popular plays, please visit our website:

www.insightpublications.com.au

www.ingramcontent.com/pod-product-compliance
Lightning Source LLC
Chambersburg PA
CBHW070551170426
43201CB00012B/1806